Temple Musical Instruments of Kerala

L.S. Rajagopalan

Edited by
A. Purushothaman
A. Harindranath

Sangeet Natak Akademi
New Delhi

D.K. Printworld (P) Ltd.
New Delhi

Front Cover: Musicians play the Maddaḷam and Cheṅgila — drums and gong — to announce a Kṛṣṇāṭṭam performance at the Guruvayur temple in Kerala. *Back cover*: The *gopīvastrāpaharaṇam* episode from the Kṛṣṇāṭṭam play *Kāliyamardanam* enacted at Guruvayur. The accompanying musicians are seen playing the Maddaḷam, Iṭakka, and Cheṅgila. *Photographs by A. Harindranath.*

Cataloging in Publication Data — DK
[Courtsey: D.K. Agencies (P) Ltd. <docinfo@dkagencies.com>]

Rajagopalan, L.S., 1922–2008.
Temple musical instruments of Kerala / L.S. Rajagopalan.
p. cm.
Includes bibliographical references (p.).
ISBN 13: 9788124605448 ISBN 10: 8124605440

1. Musical instruments — India — Kerala. 2. Musical instruments Religious aspects — Hinduism. 3. Folk music — India — Kerala. 4. Temples, Hindu — India — Kerala. I. Title.

DDC 784.1745095483 22

ISBN 13: 978-81-246-0544-8 **ISBN 10: 81-246-0544-0**
First published in India in 2010

Published by:
Sangeet Natak Akademi
Rabindra Bhavan, Feroze Shah Road, New Delhi - 110 001
Phones : (011) 2338 7246; 2338 7248; *Fax* : (011) 2338 2659
E-mail : sangeetnatak@bol.net.in

and

D.K. Printworld (P) Ltd.
Regd. office : *'Srikunj,'* F-52, Bali Nagar, New Delhi - 110 015
Phones : (011) 2545 3975; 2546 6019; *Fax* : (011) 2546 5926
E-mail: indology@dkprintworld.com; *Web*: www.dkprintworld.com

Foreword

L.S. RAJAGOPALAN was widely known as a treasure house of information on many art subjects like Kūṭiyāṭṭam, Kathakali, Kṛṣṇāṭṭam, Veda chanting, etc. L.S.R., as he was known among his friends and admirers, has been a *guru* and guide to a large number of students and researchers in the field of performing arts of Kerala during the last fifty years. The present book is a collection of his articles published in different journals, covering a wide range of topics, connected with temple and folk musical instruments and the artistic legacies of Kerala.

Most of these articles were written as texts of lecture-demonstrations of the musical instruments held at the annual conferences of the Madras Music Academy and published in its journal during 1967-77. Enriched by legends, tales and anecdotes, these writings give a wealth of information about Kerala's arts and provide an inspiring exposure to the musical culture of the region.

Right from the references from *Nāṭyaśāstra* and *Śilappadikāram*, the age-old authoritative texts dealing with Indian aesthetics, the author has enumerated all the divisions of *ghanaṁ* (solid or idiophone), *avanaddhaṁ* (membrophonic); *suṣiraṁ* (aerophonic or wind); and *tataṁ* (chordophonic or string) *vādya*s of the region. While dealing with the rhythm instruments, he reflects on a very relevant fact about the dearth of melodic instruments in the Kerala musical tradition. The stringed musical tool of the folk variety known as *puḷḷuvan vīṇā* is the only one of its kind, with a single string made from a particular creeper, creating a peculiar muffled drone to accompany the ritualistic songs related to serpent worship. There are two other *tata vādya*s (chordophonic variety), *nantuṇi* and *puḷḷuvan kuṭam*, both belonging to the plucking type, which create a tonal and rhythmic support to vocal music.

We find only a very limited number of *suṣira* (aerophonic) *vādya*s like *kompu* and *kuḻal*, both being used mostly to support the rhythm ensembles by giving a melodic flow.

Śaṅkha (conch) stands unique as a *suṣira vādya* to produce an auditory effect of highly auspicious nature. It helps also to create a ritual thrust of dramatic dimension. In the article on *kompu vādyam*, the references to wind instruments in the *Mahābhārata* and *Bhāgavata* are presented.

The place of rhythm instruments both *ghanaṁ* (idiophone) as well as *avanaddhaṁ* (membrophone) is unique in the Kerala musical system and this fact is amply suggested by the author in the naming of his book as *Temple Musical Instruments of Kerala*. None of the string and wind varieties has transcended its folk limitations or nuances to develop into highly classical level of expression. However, the cardinal musical quality of the region demonstrates itself in the obviously interesting mixing of the subtle and gross sound patterns in an instrument like *iṭakka*. The etymological details about the nomenclature and the mythical beliefs connected with this *devavādya* are dealt with at length which indeed would provide a treat for the reader.

When the *pūjā* is performed inside the sanctum sanctorum of the temple, the *sopāna* singer stands on the side of the *sopānam* (the stair which leads to the inner chamber) and sings the special musical compositions meant for each *pūjā* to the accompaniment of *iṭakka*. The compositions known as *tyāṇi*s are set to specific *rāga*s which are suited for the time of the day or night when the *pūjā* is performed inside the sanctum. The *rāga*s selected for these occasions are known as *samaya rāga*s. There is an interesting article in this collection which deals briefly with the history of *tāḷa-vādya*s. Here he tries to relate the folk-ritual background of these instruments to the divine Mother Goddess in her terrible form and the tāntric nature of the worship. The techniques involved in the playing of *cheṇṭa*; the specialities of the *laya-vinyāsa* in slowly increasing the speed in the percussion ensembles like *tāyampaka*, the languages of the instruments involved therein and the system of teaching are all extensively dealt with.

The unique features of *miḻāvu*, a percussion instrument of antiquity used in Kūṭṭu and Kūṭiyāṭṭam, are elaborately described with all details about the purificatory ceremony which the chākyār (traditional actor) has to undergo before he makes his debut as an actor and the initiation rituals done for the *miḻāvu*. The Indian belief that human body is regarded as a musical instrument is amply justified in the concept of *gātra vīṇā*, which testifies the ability of human beings to produce music through the voice. The idea that human body is a dwelling with nine holes (*navadvāravasatī*) is an analogy of philosophic dimension. When the author explains the mnemonics (*suṣkākṣara*s) of the musical instruments, it is established that each instrument is characterized by its own particular features which mark the respective linguistic nuances.

While mentioning about the *sopānam* system of music Rajagopalan vehemently argues the neccessity to redeem the rare and defunct *rāga*s like *naḷatta, śrīkaṇṭhi, sāmantamalahari,* etc. which were once popular in Kerala's temple music. Similarly the different *tāḷa*s special to Kerala and regularly practised and preserved in the musical ensembles are also defined. These rhythms include *chempaṭa* (8 *mātrā*s), *aṭanta* (14), *muṟiaṭanta* (7), *pañchāri* (6), *chempa* (10), *eka* (1).

Here it may be mentioned that apart from the above *tāḷa*s which are often played in all the major rhythm ensembles, Kerala had been able to preserve its traditional rhythms based on the *mārgī* system as laid down in the *Nāṭyaśāstra*. This is the method of practising the *pāta* (*saśabda*) and the *kalā* (the *aśabda* — non-sound). This simple rhythm principle lies deep in the folk and ritualistic arts of the common people of Kerala as expressed in Teyyam, Arjunanirtham, Paṭayaṇi, etc. The rhythms which are referred to by Rajagopalan as practised in the instrumental ensembles also belong to this *mārgī* source, and their ramified use by permutation and combination of the *mātrā*s of *pāta* and *kalā* provides a rich variety of rhythm patterns among which Kuñchan Nambiar had identified a few, in his Tuḷḷal works, with specific names for each.

They are *kārika, pañchāri* (*ayyati*), *chempaṭa, chempa, aṭanta, muṟiaṭanta, marmam, kuṇṭanāchchi, kumbham* and *lakṣmī*. But basing on the *pāta-kalā* interaction we find a number of such rhythms which do not have any name, but at the same time do have their own character and specialty. *Teyyam* is the major ritual form which evinces the richness in such rhythm structures.

L.S.R. has given us a very valuable insight into the potentials of a regional art culture and I would like — as L.S.R. did — to request all concerned people, temple authorities, cultural organizations and the government to initiate and sustain activities to preserve and propagate our rich and intangible art heritage for the betterment of our social life. Sangeet Natak Akademi is proud to present this work to lovers of the rich and vibrant *bṛhaddeśī* tradition of our country.

'Hari Sri,' Aramada
Thiruvananthapuram **Kavalam Narayana Panikkar**

A Note from the Editors

OUR acquaintance with L.S. Rajagopalan occurred only towards the end of his long life, but it quickly grew into a warm friendship. It was in 2003 that his name came up in a discussion with Rustom Bharucha, the well-known theatre scholar, in Calcutta. Dr Bharucha spoke enthusiastically of Sri Rajagopalan's intimate knowledge of Kṛṣṇāṭṭam, and as that was (and has remained) our principal interest among the performing arts of Kerala, we made up our mind to meet Rajagopalan on our next trip home. We met him for the first time in February of 2004. Later, we would look him up every year at his house in Thrissur — Lakshmi Nivas — when we were visiting Guruvayur to watch Kṛṣṇāṭṭam performances at the temple.

The idea of putting together this book emerged in the course of our initial meetings. Rustom Bharucha had, again, suggested that LSR's articles in various periodicals could be compiled and published in book form, and had also remarked that, given the range of Rajagopalan's intimate knowledge of the arts of Kerala, such a publication would be a boon to scholars. LSR himself came forward with the idea of selecting for the book those of his writings that deal with the instruments played in the temples of Kerala — instruments unique to Kerala, producing a music resonant with the life of the land.

We then began the process of putting the book together, obtaining copies of relevant articles from Rajagopalan. While we made only minimal textual changes in these pieces, we did add on diacritical marks to help readers outside Kerala. We then went over the references to texts on music in the articles, re-checked them all, and prepared the bibliography and index. Line drawings of the instruments, beautifully prepared by Manikandan Punnakkal of Thrissur, were added at the suggestion of Dr Martha Ashton Sikora, the American scholar of Kṛṣṇāṭṭam and Rajagopalan's informal student. It was finally our (self-imposed) task to type the entire text and prepare a roughly formated copy in electronic form, along with illustrations. That was the 'manuscript' sent to Sangeet Natak Akademi, now before readers in book form. It is a pity that the author is no longer present to receive the book from us, as our tribute to his lifelong work in the arts of Kerala.

Besides LSR, we are deeply indebted to a number of persons for their help in the making of this book. Dr Martha Ashton Sikora provided constant encouragement and read the re-typed essays. Sri Manikandan Punnakkal, at Martha's suggestion, prepared the illustrations. Sri P. Radhakrishnan Nair of Guruvayur clarified the meanings of words in medieval Malayalam works which have been referred to in the text. Dr A. Krishnadas of Kalpetta readily recited and provided the text of the song *Kamini Mani* composed by Swati Tirunal. Dr P.N. Ganesh of Thrissur held many helpful discussions with us, while Dr T.N. Vasudevan, also of Thrissur, clarified the meanings of many words. We must especially thank Sri Kavalam Narayana Panikkar, the former Vice-Chairman of Sangeet Natak Akademi (2004-09), for his keen interest in publishing the book and for contributing a foreword to it. We also thank Sri Jayant Kastuar and Sri Abhijit Chatterjee of Sangeet Natak Akademi, New Delhi, for considering the compilation for publication and bringing our proposal to fruition. Last but not least, Sri Abhijit Chatterjee suggested the photographs used on the front and back covers of the book and improved the presentation of this note from the editors.

Acknowledgements need to be made, before we sign out, to the periodicals where these articles first appeared. The largest number comes from the *Journal of the Music Academy*, Madras: "Cheṇṭa" and "A brief history of the tāla vādyas of Kerala" were published in that journal under the title "Thayambaka" (Vol. XXXVIII, pp 83-102, 1967); "Timila" was published under the title "Thimila" in Volume XLII (pp. 165-71, 1971); "Śuddha maddaḷam" was published under the title "The Suddha Maddala of Kerala" (Vol. XLIII, pp. 119-33, 1972); "Kompu vādyam" was published under the title "Kombu Vadya of Kerala" (Vol. XLIV, pp. 170-77, 1973); "Miḻāvu" was published under the title "The Mizhavu" (Vol. XLV, pp. 109-17. 1974); "Kuṟum kuḻal" was published under the title "The Kurum Kuzhal of Kerala" (Vol. XLVI, pp. 144-57, 1975); "Iṭakka" was published under the title "Idakka" (Vol. XLVIII, pp. 165-70, 1977); and "Pulluvans and their Music" was published in Volume LI (pp. 72-80, 1980). "Ilattāḷam" appeared under the title "Injhan Jinjhan Jhee" in the *Thrissur Pooram Souvenir* of 1988 published by the Tiruvambady Devaswom. "Folk Musical Instruments of Kerala" and "Bhagavati Pāttu of the Mannans" were published in *Sangeet Natak*, the journal of Sangeet Natak Akademi (No. 33, pp. 40-45, 1974, and Vol. XXXIX, pp. 18-22, 2005 respectively). We thank the editors of these periodicals for granting permission to reproduce the articles.

A. Purushothaman
A. Harindranath

December, 2009

Contents

1

Iṭakka

IṬAKKA is a small drum which is inseparable from the rituals of Kerala temples. References to this instrument can be seen even in the oldest of Malayalam literature. It is considered to be a very auspicious instrument — a *devavādyam*.

The name *iṭakka* obviously seems to be derived from the name *ḍakka,* the prefix I (E) having been added as in the usual procedure adopted in Tamil, like *irāman* for *rāman*. The *Saṅgīta Ratnākara* of Śārṅgadeva describes three instruments of similar design, the *huḍukka*, the *ḍakka* and the *maṇḍi ḍakka* and probably *iṭakka* would be a developed form of *maṇḍi ḍakka*. *Iṭakka* consists of a wooden barrel to

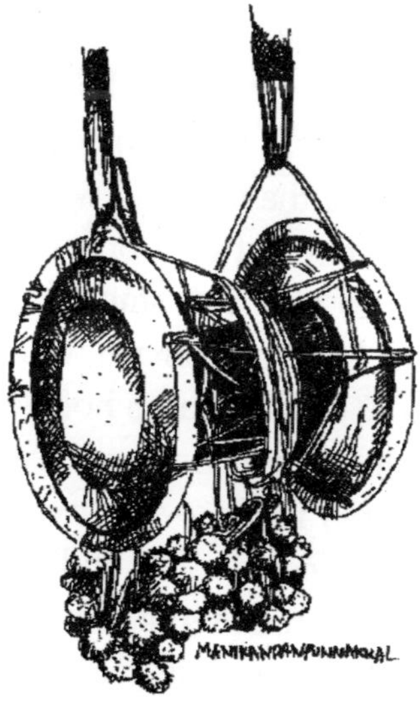

Iṭakka

Iṭakka Artist

which are attached two pieces of thin hide fixed on two wooden rings, these being held tight with cotton tapes. Four pegs are inserted between the ropes at the bottom to keep them taut and in proper position. The wooden barrel is normally made of *karuṅgāli* (*Acacia catechu*) or *rakta chandana* (red sanders) or Jackwood. It is about 8 to 8½ inches long and the diameter of the face is 4 to 4½ inches, the thickness of the wood being about ½ inch. The diameter is slightly smaller at the middle of the barrel and it gradually flares out towards the ends. It is to be noted that the barrel is not hour glass shaped like the *uṭukku*. Two rings of diameter of 8 to 8½ inches are cut out of a one inch thick Jackwood plank and turned to give it a smooth and proper shape. The thin hide of the internal stomach walls of a cow is pasted tight on the rings with gum and 6 holes are drilled into the rings. The two hide covered rings are fixed on either end of the barrel with cotton ropes — the twist of the rope being important to give proper tension and ease of handling. At the end of the barrel on either side two small copper nails are fixed diametrically opposite each other — total four on each end. Two palmyrah fibres are tied to these across the face of the barrel on each side. The hide will be just touching the fibres when the rings are tightened. So when the face is struck, it gives a vibrating sound similar to the snare of the snare drum. Four wooden pegs turned in a lathe to give a fancy design about seven inches long and one inch diameter are inserted between the ropes holding the rings. These pegs are called *jīva kōl*. Sixteen multicoloured woolen balls-tassels are hung from each *jīva kōl*. The total of 64 such balls probably represent the 64 arts (*chatuṣṣaṣṭi kala*). A thin stick made of Tamarind wood or *chappaṅgam* (*Caesalpinia sappan* Linn) or even horn is used for playing. The instrument is hung from the left shoulder by means of straps and it is played only in a standing posture. While the instrument is played with the stick held in the right hand, the left hand holds the barrel — by a strap wound round the barrel — and pushes it up and down. The downward movement increases the tension and an upward one decreases it. This produces a wide variation in the tone and the *iṭakka* is one of the rare instruments in which it is the barrel that is moved for altering the tension of the hides to produce tonal variations.

Beginner's Lessons

As in the case of some other instruments also, the student starts learning to play on a dummy before he starts playing on a real instrument. The dummy here is only a small rectangular piece of wood covered with leather and stuffed with a bit of cotton on one side. This piece — called *kayyatta* is held in the palm by the thumb and finger, the cotton stuffed side being next to the palm. A six-inch long, thick stick shaped like a club is held in the right hand the fist almost touching the thigh. Some two or three learner's lessons are practised in four speeds — *ta ki ṭa, ta ri ki ṭa,* etc., etc. These lessons are then practised on the *iṭakka,* the left hand manipulating the barrel so as to produce the different tones as per mnemonics. A set piece known as *Gaṇapati Kai* is learnt (*kita dhika dhen ku them, kita dhika dhenkuku thaku, thakr thakr dhem dhem kuku,* etc., etc.). This is first played whenever a player starts to play the *iṭakka* as an audio offering to Lord Gaṇeśa, the remover of all obstacles. The student then practises different types of set patterns of playing called *kūṟu* which are to be played for various *pūjā*s — different sets being played according to the time of the day, just as different *rāga*s are prescribed for different periods of a day.

A community of temple servants called *mārār*s and in some of the northern regions of Kerala, the *potuvāḷ*s, are traditionally entitled to play the instrument in the temple, a family being attached to a temple. Unfortunately due to Land Reforms, the revenues of temples have dwindled to almost nothing. The *miṟāsī* rights of these temple servants bring them hardly any income and they neglect this art and take to other avocations.

The *iṭakka* is never kept on the ground. It is invariably hung from a peg or a rafter in the temple. And thereby hangs a tale. The *iṭakka* was one of the instruments used by Viṣṇu. Once the Śivagaṇas stole it and started playing it during Lord Śiva's dance. Thereupon Lord Śiva chided them and ordered them to return it back to Viṣṇu. When Śivagaṇas went to Viṣṇu, He refused to take it back and sent them back with a curse saying that if they placed it down somewhere, the whole ground around it would explode.

In the *Saṅgīta Ratnākara* it is mentioned that the *devatā* of *ḍakka* is Vindhyāvāsinī (Bhagavatī) and that it is used during her worship in rendering ritualistic songs (*charyagāna*). The *iṭakka* is used in all temples of Kerala (funds permitting of course) and it is also used in the ritualistic Sanskrit drama of Kerala — The Kūṭiyāṭṭam.

The main function of *iṭakka* is for playing in the temple during *pūjā* time. When *pūjā* is done with closed doors it is the custom to sing to the accompaniment of *iṭakka*. The *mārā*rs are normally good singers — the famous Ṣaṭkāla Govinda Mārār who was supposed to have been instrumental in Saint Tyāgarāja singing *entaro mahānubhāvulu* was one of their tribe. During the rituals connected with temple festivals (*viḷakku-āchāram*), *iṭakka* is particularly important in one of the circumambulations called *iṭakka pradakṣiṇam*. A number of instruments were used for a sort of orchestra effect and this has later developed into the modern *pañchavādyam*[1] which is one of the most delightful ensembles of instruments of Kerala including the *iṭakka*. Because of its low sound volume it is usually drowned in the boom of the other instruments like *timila, maddaḷam,* etc. But when there is a competitive improvization (similar to *tani āvarttanam*) between *maddaḷam, timila,* etc., *iṭakka* is an instrument to be reckoned with for its delicate nuances especially in the hands of some experts.

In Kathakali, the *iṭakka* is played when a female character holds the stage (when the *cheṇṭa* is not played). In Kūṭiyāṭṭam, the *iṭakka* gives good support to the pot drum

1. S. Venkita Subramania Iyer, "The Panhcavadyam", *Journal of the Madras Music Academy,* (1957).

— the *miḻāvu*. In fact, *iṭakka*, which is most suitable as accompaniment for various dance forms, has already become a regularly accepted member of the orchestra of several dance troupes even outside Kerala and it has also attracted several Westerners to it. *Sopāna Saṅgīta* which is claimed to be a specialty of Kerala is intimately connected with the *iṭakka*. There has been a lot of controversy and unnecessary heat generated as to what exactly is *sopāna saṅgīta* or *sopāna mārga* of *saṅgīta*. Without entering into those controversies we shall confine our attention to the music sung at the *sopāna* of the temples. The tonal variations capable of being produced on the *iṭakka* comes in handy for the singing. During *pūjā* time, devotional songs are sung standing near the steps leading to the sanctum and this is the right of the *mārār* and the accompaniment is the *iṭakka*. If there be more than one singer, a *Cheṅgila* is also used. To begin with *tṛsthāna* is first sounded on the *iṭakka*, *sa-pa-sa*. Then nāṭṭa *rāga* is played on the *iṭakka* or it is sung to the accompaniment of the *iṭakka*. Then invocatory songs are sung to the gods. These are called *tyāṇi* (from *dhyāna*) songs. Songs on Gaṇeśa and Sarasvatī are first sung, then others on the deity of the temple. After this some *kīrtana*s and/or *aṣṭapadi*s of Jayadeva are sung. In between the stanzas of the songs a finale or *muttāyippu* is played on the *iṭakka*.

Tyāṇis

These were being sung in some old *rāga*s which have not only gone out of vogue but also have become practically unknown. There are a few old men here and there who are capable of singing these at least in outline. The following are the names of some of these special *rāga*s: *naḷatta, śrīkāṇṭhi, pūvāli, andhāḷi, muḍḍan, sāmanta malahari, antari*. It is significant that the names of the modes (*svaras* as they are called) in *Kūṭiyāṭṭam* also bear the names *śrīkāṇṭhi, muḍḍan* and *antari.*[2] If some experts study the singing of these old modes sung by these *mārārs*, it may be possible to salvage some of the *rāgas*.

Aṣṭapadis

The *rāgas* used in singing *aṣṭapadis* in Kerala are not always what are prescribed in the texts. The singing of *aṣṭapadis* is not confined to Viṣṇu temples alone. They are sung in all temples — Śiva, Bhagavatī, Śāsta or Viṣṇu. Some of the *rāgas* current in Kathakali music like *dvijāvanti, ghaṇṭāram, poṟanīr, pāṭi,* etc. are used in singing some *aṣṭapadis* also.

In the matter of selecting *rāgas* for different periods of the day, the pattern observed by them generally conforms to that observed elsewhere in south India.

Uṣaḥ pūjā	4 a.m.	*poṟanīr, bhūpāḷam*
Morning *pūjā*	6 a.m.	*desākṣī, bilahari, śrīkaṇṭhi*
Pantīraṭi	8.30 a.m.	*naḷatta, pūvāḷi*
Midday	11 a.m.	*śrī rāga*
Afternoon (only in very few temples)	3.30 p.m.	*mohanam, kalyāṇi*
Sunset		*nāṭṭa, sāveri*
Night		*sāveri, kāmbhoji, śaṅkarābharaṇam*

2. L.S. Rajagopalan, "Music in Kootiyattam", *Sangeet Natak*, 10, pp. 12-25, (1968).

It is possible that some of the *tyāṇi* songs and *kīrtana*s were composed by *mārār*s themselves. A story about a *mārār* of *mūkkōla* temple who could compose verses impromptu is popular.

It is said that once Uddaṇḍa Śāstri visited the temple at *mūkkōla*[3] and began to compose a verse in honour of the deity there. After composing the first half of the verse

> *saṁbharita bhūri kṛpamaṁba śubhamaṅgam*
> *śuṁbatu cirantanamidaṁ tava madantaḥ* ।

he was thinking how to complete it in the same style, when a *mārār* who was playing instrumental music on the *iṭakka* completed it thus:[4]

> *jaṁbharipu kuṁbhivara kuṁbha yuga ḍaṁbha-*
> *staṁbhikuca kuṁbha pariraṁbha para śaṁbhuḥ* ।

It may be noted that the rhythm of the verse echoes the playing of the *iṭakka* in temples.

Local poets also might have contributed by composing songs on the deities of their native temples. In Malabar area some songs composed by members of the Zamorins Royal family are current. They have the *mudrā*s, the name of the composer, Manavikrama or Manaveda in the *charaṇa*s.

It is the practice in Kerala in some temples and in some aristocratic houses to perform *kaḷam pūjā*. *Kaḷam* is a drawing of a deity done on the floor with five coloured powders, rice, turmeric, *kumkumam*, green leaf and

---

3. L.S. Rajagopalan, "Siva Giti of Ramapanivada", *Journal of the Madras Music Academy*, (1965).

4. K. Kunjunni Raja, *The Contribution of Kerala to Sanskrit Literature*, p. 73.

charcoal. *Pūjā* is done and special songs called *toṟṟam* songs are sung and an oracle goes into trance and dances. The deities so worshipped are Bhagavatī, Veṭṭakkorumakan (Lord Śiva as a Hunter), Ayyappan, etc. For these *pūjā*s also *iṭakka* is sometimes used.

Playing of Rāgas and Songs on the Iṭakka

Due to the rich tonal variations — nearly two octaves — it is possible to play *varṇa*s and *kīrtana*s on the *iṭakka*. A few experts have developed this technique. Due to the inherent shortcomings of a percussion instrument, there are limitations to its being used as a solo instrument but as a *pakkavādya*, it would serve excellently. There is vast scope for developing *iṭakka* on these lines. One can play all the mnemonics of a *mṛdaṅga* on the *iṭakka*. In music concerts today, one often hears a mṛdaṅgist trying to imitate all the *svara* patterns sung by the vocalist, on the *mṛdaṅga*. This can be done perfectly on the *iṭakka*. For a delicate instrument like the *vīṇā*, it will even be a better *tāḷa* accompaniment than a *mṛdaṅga*.

The *iṭakka* is the most delicately versatile among the many percussion instruments of Kerala.

2

Ilattāḷam

Bharata Muni's *Nāṭyaśāstra* is the oldest treatise we have on music and dance. In this famous work, musical instruments have been divided into four classes, viz. *tataṁ* (chordophones), *avanaddhaṁ* (membrophones), *ghanaṁ* (idiophones) and *suṣiraṁ* (aerophones), which in common parlance become stringed instruments like *vīṇā*, violin, etc.; instruments covered with skins like drum, *cheṇṭa*, etc.; solid instruments like gongs and cymbals; and wind instruments like flute, *nāgasvaram*, etc. No better classification has been possible and Westerners also accept this scheme, though a new type of instruments has come up in the electronic field which only imitate these four types. We shall consider here the cymbals used in Kerala.

The most commonly used instrument is the *ilattāḷam*. It is known as *brahma tāḷam* in Sanskrit. The normal instrument consists of a pair of bell metal discs about six inches in diameter with a hemispherical depression in the middle.

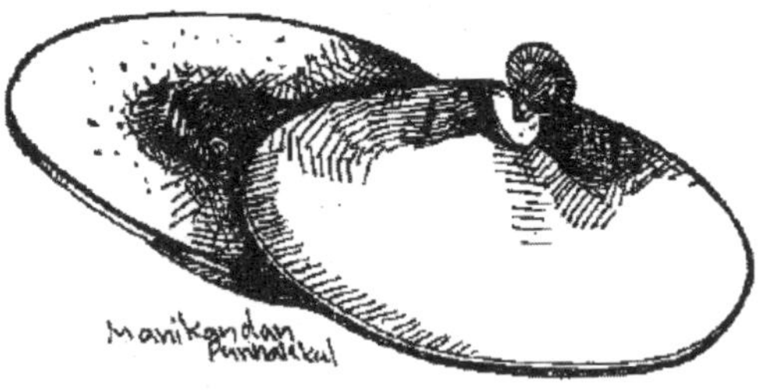

Ilattāḷam

Through a hole in its centre, a thick string is introduced and a knot is tied on the other end to prevent it from slipping out. One disc is held in either hand and played by clanging them together. The clang produces a resonant vibration which lasts for quite some time and during this period the top disc is gently slid over the lower disc which gives a vibratory effect called *tarippu*. One common mnemonics for the sound (*vāyttāri*) is *injanjhiiiii injanjhiiii injhan jhanjhanjhiii*.

The composition of the bell metal, the size of the instrument and above all the heat treatment, etc. contribute to the vibratory effect. The bell metal pieces are first cast and they are specially heat treated and forged. The "heating and hammering" contribute much to the quality of the instrument. The *Saṅgīta Ratnākara* — another Sanskrit treatise on music — mentions particularly about this heat treatment.

While *ilattāḷam* is mainly used as a "time marker" for ensembles of other instruments, it adds greatly to the charm of the orchestra by playing suitable cross rhythms. Often it is the ring of these cymbals that is heard first when one approaches a group playing *cheṇṭa meḷam* or *pañchavādyam*. A combination of muting (stopping the vibrations with the fingers) and extended ringing (*tarippu*) is used to give proper effect. Although it normally occupies only a secondary position in the drum ensembles (*cheṇṭa meḷam* or *pañchavādyam*, etc.), there are a few artists who can play solo — a *tāyampaka* or *tani āvarttanam* and bring it to the level of a virtuoso instrument. It would be in the fitness of things if such solo performances of artists are encouraged.

In this connection, a demonstration given at the Mani Iyer Memorial Percussion Art Centre at Bangalore in the year 1987 comes to mind. An artist from Bījāpur gave a demonstration on the *kartāḻ*, a pair of hemispherical cymbals, one slightly smaller than the other. The audience including many veteran *mṛdaṅga* players and musicians were amazed at the playing. In fact, the artist could reproduce all the *bol*s (*vāyttāri*) of the *tabala* on his cymbals. The artist was so poor that he could not afford to get a pair made in bell metal, but was using a pair made of cast iron. A time was, say fifty years ago, when the cost of an *ilattāḷam* was only a fraction of what it is now, several of the artists could not own an instrument of their own. In those days, no artist who volunteered to play in the temple of Mahārājā of Cochin at Tripunithura was turned away. Taking advantage of this patronage, a few poor fellows in dire circumstances used to offer their services. As they could not afford to get these instruments they would make dummy instruments cut from arecanut flower sheaths (*pāḷa*) and they would colour them appropriately. They would make up for the absence of the real instruments with the physical action of their head, hand and torso. The supervising authorities would also turn a blind eye on these poor fellows so as not to deny them a few days food and wages.

Formerly proper attention was being paid in selecting all *ilattāḷam*s used in an ensemble to a uniform *śruti* (pitch). Unfortunately that aspect is being neglected. Sometimes one hears a cacophony of sounds and even cracked cymbals are used whose sound is jarring. A pair of *ilattāḷam* weighs more than a kilo. The high cost of bell metal and high wages of the *mūśāri* (bell metal artisan) are to some extent responsible for this sorry state of affairs. However the managements of temples can now well afford to get a dozen or more sets of *ilattāḷams* with matched *śrutis* made for use in the festivals.

The making of an instrument is a science as well as an art. The number of artisans are dwindling. Katavallur in National Highway No. 17 near Trichur, is still a centre for this. It is the duty of the temple authorities to take a keen interest in the manufacture of these instruments and help its proper revival.

3

Kur̲um Kul̲al

The *kur̲um kul̲al,* also called *kul̲al,* is one of the musical instruments traditionally used in temple-worship in Kerala. It belongs to the class of *suṣira vādyas* or wind instruments. It is a double reeded pipe — a dimunitive *nāgasvaram* — and is almost the same as the *śehnāī* of the north and the *mukha-vīṇā* of the south.

The instrument may be 12 to 18 inches long. It consists of a conical wooden pipe called *oḷavu* with a metal bell bottom attachment called *kīl̲aṇaśu.* At the top end the reed (*nar̲ukku*) is fixed a small metal top attachment called *mēl̲aṇaśu.* In some instruments there will not be a top attachment since that portion will also be turned out of the

Kul̲al

same piece of wood as the tube. The bottom attachment may also be of wood. The need is made by a detailed process from a reed plant growing wild in marshy places. This is fixed to a small tube called *nelli* which is inserted at the top of the pipe to fit properly. Formerly a circular metal or horn or mother of pearl disc called *kaviḷiṭikki* used to be fixed at the end of the reed. This disc is rarely seen nowadays. This disc is said to help — quite correctly I should think — even toothless artists play properly. Spare reeds, a horn or ivory bodekin (to clear the reeds) are hung from a string connecting the top and bottom attachments. It has seven holes in one line and there is one more hole at the top on the lower side which is closed by the left thumb.

The word *kuḻal* (*kuzhal*) means a tube both in Malayālam and Tamil. In musical parlance *kuḻal* means a musical instrument. To differentiate instruments, names like *Oṭak-kuḻal* (flute), *kuṟum kuḻal* (short pipe), etc. are given. *Kuḻal* is mentioned even in one of the earliest Malayālam works, the *Rāmakatha pāṭṭu* of the fourteenth century.[1] Kuñchan Nambiar in his Tuḷḷal works mentions the name *kuṟum kuḻal* itself along with other instruments including *nāgasvaram*.[2] The expressions *koṭṭum kuḻalum* and *kompum kuḻalum* are

1. *Rāmakathapāṭṭu* of Ayyapilla Asan, Ayodhyā Kāṇḍam, Viruttam 3, Pāṭṭ 10.
2. The Tuḷḷal work of Kuñchan Nāmbiar, Pradoṣa Māhātmyam:

   kaṭupiṭayuḷḷoru tappum takilum
   kompu kuṟum kuḻal nāgasvaravum

   It is to be noted that both *kuṟum kuḻal* and *nāgasvaram* are mentioned separately. In his Sabhā Praveśam, Kuñchan Nāmbiar says:

→

often seen in literature as well as spoken language. *Kuḻal* is also mentioned in *Śilappadikāram,* the famous Tamil epic.

This type of double reed pipes is found all over the world, but, when a Keralite considers the process of its development, he gets nostalgic memories of the toy *pīppi* made from coconut palm-leaf by children. A one inch bit of coconut palm-leaf is folded length-wise. The two halves are manipulated to take a slightly curved shape so that the ends would be elliptical. This would serve as a toy reed and when long bits of palm-leaf are wound round this, to make a conical tube, the child gets a good toy whistle. This toy is further developed by fixing the leaf reed to the circular leaf stem of a papaya plant. Some holes are also made on the tubular stem to produce different notes!

We see the next development in the *kuḻal* used by the Paṟaya community in Kerala.[3] The reed is made of four bits of palm-leaf (Palmyrah). In the instruments normally available in Trichur district, the stem is a conical tube made of any jungle wood and is about 6 inches long and 1 inch in diameter at the bottom. A thin bell-metal bell attached to this is about 4 inches long and has a diameter of 4¼ inches at the end. The bottom-most hole is 2 inches from the end of the wooden tube. There are 4 more holes and the distance between each is being gradually reduced. There is a coconut shell disc lip-guard between the top hole and

→ *pāṇṭimeḷamuruṭṭucheṇṭa kuṟumkuḻal iṭitāḷavum*
tittimaddaḷaveṇuvīṇkaḷ timila takil mukhavīṇayum

He mentions both *kuṟum kuḻal* and *mukha-vīṇā.*

3. The Paṟayas are traditional basket makers and also suppliers of raw hide from dead animals. They usually supply the skins required for drum, etc.

the reed called *kaviḷāṭi.* The bell is called *kuḻal tāḷam.* There is no top attachment but the reed is fixed to a small metal tube (*nelli*) and fixed to the top with strings in a crude way.

They play this pipe for their social functions like the attainment of puberty of girls, death ceremonies, for festivals like buffalo race, "Dance with a Headgear" (Muṭiyāṭṭam), the Oracle (Veḷichchapāṭu) dance in Devī temples, etc. They have some songs which they sing in a peculiar mode appropriate to the occasion and the notes produced in their *kuḻal* correspond to these chants. A trained ear can easily distinguish the different modes of these chants. The following *svara*s are heard: *sa ga ma pa ga ma pa dha pa ma pa ga.* While they produce only some 3 or 4 notes on their *kuḻal* it has a weird, eerie or haunting effect, especially when one hears it at night. The 5 holes in this primitive instrument remind one of the pentatonic scale in the development of music.

There is another folk instrument known as *īḻava vādyam* which is seen in the Tenmalappuram area of Pālghāṭ district, where there is a good deal of Tamilian influence. As the name suggests the instrument is played by the Īḻava community and it is used for some social functions and for rituals and festivals in Kāḷī Temples. A normal instrument has a conical wooden tube about 13 inches long, with bottom diameter about ¾ inch. The bell metal bottom attachment is called *kāḷam* (corruption for *kāhaḷam*) which is about 4 inches long with its bottom diameter also about 4 inches. The top metal attachment is called *mēlaṇi* and is about 2½ inches long. There are seven playing holes plus four more vent holes at the bottom. Mandara wood (*Bauhinia purpures*) is claimed to be the best. Black wood and palmyrah wood are also seen. The reed used to be made of palm-leaf but now only *nāgasvaram* reeds are used. The tube of a *timiri nāgasvaram* is sometimes used now since the demand for a new instrument is almost nil and no one seems to know how to make it. Their practice lessons are called *charaḷi* but they do not identify the *svaras* as *sa ri ga ma*, etc. The students learn from observation of the demonstration of the *guru*. After learning the *charaḷi* in which there are some 12 lessons they learn to play some pieces which they call *chiṇṭu*. Normally half tones are not produced, but of late they have started rendering film songs. The drum accompaniment is called *tavil* (which is a bit different from the normal *tavil* of Tamil Nadu). They do not use *ottu* or *śruti*. A team consists of 2 to 3 pipers, one drummer and one *ilattāḷam* player.

The *kuṟum kuḻal* is normally played by the Nair community in Kerala. Some families have been pipers for generations at some of the temples and many of them have the honorific title of Paṇikkar which is normally the equivalent of an Army Sergeant or drill master. Some references are seen about the use of *kuḻal* during the marching of the Army. The fact that the Nair community which is noted for its military traditions is playing it and that the players are called Paṇikkar goes to show its martial tradition.

In Kerala there are a few special castes known as Ambalavāsis or temple servants, like the Mārār, the Piṣāroṭi, Vārrier, etc. The Mārārs are the traditional drummers and musicians in the temple and for some of the most important rituals they play the instruments like *śaṅkha, cheṅgila, pāṇi maram, iṭakka, cheṇṭa* and *timila*. There is no place for instruments like *kuḻal* or *kompu* during these rituals like Śrī Bhūta Bali, etc. As such one is led to the conclusion that the *kulal* and *kompu* were in fact foreign instruments which later got absorbed into the temple service in Kerala. The *kulal* is used now in some of the temples — for *palli unarttal*, for *sevā* three times a day, for Śīveli or circumambulations with the *Utsava Vigraha* (called *Tiṭambu*), for *Chenṭa Meḷam* during elephant procession, during festivals and also for *Kūṭiyāṭṭam* — the traditional Sanskrit stage of Kerala.

An instrument called *madhukarī*[4] is described in the *Saṅgīta Ratnākara* of Śārṅgadeva. In the 6th chapter (chapter on Musical Instruments) verses 787-793:

Madhukarīlakṣaṇam

śṛṅgajā dāravī vā syāt kāhalākṛtidhāriṇī ।
aṣṭāviṁśyataṁgulā ca dhairghyai madhukarī śubāḥ ॥

mukharandhraṁ ca tasyāḥ syāt tuvarībījasaṁnibham ।
mukharandhrādaṁgulāni tyaktvā catvāri vaṁśavat ॥

vidhāya sapta randhrāṇi kurvīta vivarāntaram ।
teṣām ca mukharandhrasya madhye 'dhobhāgasaṁsthitam ॥

madhuradhvānasiddhayai tanmukharandhre tu tāmrajā ।
nidhātavyā yavasthūlā nālikā caturaṅgulā ॥

tadūrdhvam cakrikā sthāpyā dantajā śuktijāthavā ।
randhramadhye kāśamayīṁ yadvā devanalodbhavām ॥

śuktikāṁ kiṁcidunnidramālatīkalikākṛtim ।
mṛdulāṁ kṣīrapākena kṣiptvā madhukarīṁ tataḥ ॥

vaṁśavad vādayed randhraṁ pidadhītāpyadhastanam ।
vāmāṅguṣṭāgrabhāgenetyuktam niḥśaṅkasūriṇā ॥

4. *Madhukarī* derives its name from the similarity of its sound to that of the buzzing of the honey sucking Black Beetle.

This may be translated as follows:

> A good Madhukari is 18 *aṅgula*s long (one *aṅgula* is a little more than one inch) and may be made of horn or wood and is shaped like *kāhaḷa* (conical tube). The opening at the blowing end is the size of *tuvar* (*dāl*) seed. Four inches off the mouth, 7 holes are to be made as in the flute and another hole is made on the lower side between the mouth and the first hole. For getting a sweet sound a 4 inch copper tube of the diameter of a barley seed is fixed to the mouth and on top of that a circular disc of ivory or mother of pearl is to be fixed. In the hole of the tube a reed having the shape of a partially opened jasmine bud made from *deva nala* (a reed plant) and made soft by cooking in milk is to be fixed. The *madhukarī* is to be played like a *vaṁśa* (flute). The hole in the lower side is to be closed by the left thumb.[5]

When one compares the specifications given for *madhukarī* with that of *kuṟum kuḻal* we see that they are almost identical.

The instrument used to be made in Kerala in several places like Tripunithura near Cochin and Panamana village in Pālghāṭ district, Tiruvilvamala in Trichur district, etc. Due to decline in temple finances, the temple arts also declined. And the demand for the instrument became negligible. Hence it is no longer made in Kerala. It is usually obtained from manufacturers of *nāgasvaram* in Tamil Nadu, from places like Narasingampeṭṭai in Tanjore district. Old broken *nāgasvaram*s are also cut to make *kuṟum kuḻal* now.

---

5. When the hole on the lower side is to be closed by the left thumb the method of holding is also specified automatically. This is how it is done in the case of *kuṟum kuḻal* also.

Training

Traditionally the young boy goes to help his relatives who play in the temple. He keeps the cymbals for *tāḷam*. Then he starts playing the *śruti* (*ottu*) and learns to breathe and blow at the same time. This is called *śvāsam maṟikkuka*. For this a bamboo tube is taken and blowing is practised on it.[6] *Saptasvaram*s are learnt first vocally, then on the instrument. Teaching goes on as in the case of traditional Carnatic Music, with *saptasvaram, variśai, alaṅkāram, gītam, varṇam* and *kīrtanam*. Then the student graduates to the playing of *rāga*s and *paṟṟu*. *Paṟṟu* is similar to the rendering of a Pallavī. It is described later.

With the decline in the patronage for the temple arts the income of the artists also went down very much; so much so, all *kuḻal* artists have taken to the playing of *nāgasvaram*, since it is in greater demand, especially for marriages, etc. They have neglected the *kuḻal* and this has led to a great deterioration in the standard of playing, and one can rarely come across a *kuṟum kuḻal* artist who can play it really well.

The holes in the *kuṟum kuḻal* are made to correspond to the harikāmbhoji scale. Sharper or flatter notes are rendered not only by opening or closing the holes partially but also by the adjustment of the reed in the lips, pulling it out or pushing it inside the mouth and thus effectively altering the length of the air column in the tube. The last hole (in the bottom end) is taken as the *ṣaḍja*, the solitary hole in the

---

6. When I asked one of the old artists how this breathing and blowing at the same time is learnt, he gave the naive reply that when a boy is afraid of the slaps he will get from the master, he will learn in double quick time.

lower side closed by the thumb is the *niṣāda* and the first hole (at the top end) is the upper *ṣaḍja*. So the player is handicapped when he has to play the notes below the basic *ṣaḍja*. By closing the last hole near the bell bottom, with the little finger he can get *niṣāda* and by pulling the reed out he can produce *dhaivata* and even *pañchama*.

We may now compare the *kuṟum kuḻal* with other similar instruments. As already mentioned this type of wind instrument is found in many places. We considered earlier the details of *madhukarī* as given in the *Saṅgīta Ratnākara*. The name exists in its Prākṛt or slang form in the *mōhuri* of Orissa. It is used in temple rituals and in folk dances in Orissa. The name is again further corrupted in the *mōṟi* of Mysore.

The *nāgasvaram* is a development of *madhukarī*. The name *nāgasvaram* is not mentioned in literature before the fourteenth century. There is no hole in the *nāgasvaram* in the lower side to be closed by the thumb. There are also 5 holes at the bottom in *nāgasvaram* which are for the control of air exit. The *ṣaḍja* is kept on the third hole from the top and this enables the player to render the lower notes up to *gāndhāram* even. So, what is *ṣaḍja* in the *nāgasvaram* will be *pañchama* in *kuṟum kuḻal*. As the length of the *nāgasvaram* is much greater, the pitch is lower.

The *śehnāī*[7] is almost like the *kuṟum kuḻal* in size and appearance but it does not have a thumb hole on the lower side.

---

7. In some books it is seen that *śehnāī* was introduced into India from Persia and that Nai is the name of a similar instrument in Egypt. In view of the description of *madhukarī* in *Saṅgīta Ratnākara* it would be clear that such instruments already existed in India and probably only the name *śehnāī* was imported from Persia.

MUKHA VĪṆĀ

This instrument was once popular in Tamil Nadu and it is still in use in some temples. It used to be part of the Bharata Nāṭyam Orchestra (Chinna Meḷam). In the description of this instrument got from one source, the size of a normal instrument is given as 11 inches. It has 8 holes but no thumb hole on the lower side. The last but one hole is kept as the *ṣaḍja*.[8] But in the description got from another source it is mentioned that in olden days *mukha-vīṇā* used to be about 14 inches long and that it had seven holes plus a thumb hole in the lower side and the lowest hole is taken as the *ṣaḍja*.[9] From these we can conclude that the older *mukha-vīṇā* is identical with the *kuṟum kuḻal*. *Mukha-vīṇā* is mentioned in Malayalam literature also but it is probably in areas like Trivandrum where Tamil influence is more, that the instrument was known by both the names *mukha-vīṇā* and *kuṟum kuḻal*. Traditionally the wood to be used for the tube is *karuṅgāli* (Sanskrit *khādira, Acacia Sundra,* Tamil *karuṅgāli*). Ebony and dark Rose-Wood were also used.[10]

8. The description was obtained due to the courtesy of Sri T.S. Parthasarathy who inspected the *mukha-vīṇā* available at the AIR Studios at Madras.
9. This description was obtained from S.S. Rangappa, *mukha-vīṇā vidvān* of Coimbatore through the courtesy of Tiruchy Sundaram. Sri Rangappa explains that the instrument he now uses is a modified one. The tube is made of bamboo and not weed and this gives a different timbre to the sound. He has also provided extra holes to control the exit of air.
10. Khādira wood is also recommended for other musical instruments, like the maddaḷa or mṛdaṅga.

    mardalaḥ khādiraḥ śreṣṭho hīnaḥ syādanyadārujaḥ

    (details of *maddaḷa* from *Saṅgīta Dāmodara*). It is also interesting to note that even in the Vedas, *khādira* wood is →

The reed used to be made from a plant known as *āṃa* growing in marshy places. This *āma*[11] (called *śara* in Sanskrit) is also used for some Vedic sacrificial purposes in Kerala. The reed is collected during the summer before the advent of the rains. It is dried in the shade and kept aside for a year. It is then cooked by inserting in par-boiling paddy. It is again dried and then it is cooked with some meat. It is then washed and dried. It is finally boiled with milk and washed and dried.[12] Bits are cut to size and cylindrical piece of wood is inserted inside and rubbed with a strong string or a piece of gut. It is then put in a press to give it a proper shape. Nowadays no one attempts to make it in Kerala. They get it from manufacturers in Tamil Nadu. However the proper size required for *kuṟum kuḻal* is smaller than that required for the *nāgasvaram* and what they get in Tamil Nadu is the one normally required for *nāgasvaram*. With the ill fitting reed the quality of the performance declines.

All instruments made from the cut tubes of old *nāgasvaram* do necessarily have the top and also bottom

---

→ specified for making sacrificial implements.

vilvo vā khādiro vā palāśo vā anyeṣām yajñakratūnāṁ yūpā bhavanti

11. *Āma* is called *śara* in Sanskrit. The name Śaravaṇabhava for Lord Subrahmaṇya is because he was born in a forest of Śara, reeds.

12. The cooking of the reed in milk is mentioned even in the description of *madhukarī* in the *Saṅgīta Ratnākara*. Biochemists should be particularly interested in the change brought about in the reed by this process. Scientific institutions could take up research on such procedures laid down by old masters to understand and even improve upon the process.

attachments. These are made of good bell metal. The artists always keep these metal attachments well polished and they will be glittering in the sun during elephant processions. Formerly the bell shaped attachment used to be plain in shape but now the shape is more artistic with ridges and rings around it.

The Use of Kuṟum Kuḻal in Temple Service in Kerala

1. It is used for *paḷḷi uṇarttal*, early morning between 3 and 5 a.m. It is also used for *sevā*, morning, noon, evening and night, for *dīpārādhana*, etc. Though the instrument is mostly replaced by *nāgasvaram* it can still be seen in some of the temples. The following *rāga*s are normally played according to the time of the day.

3 to 5 a.m.	*bhūpāḷam*
6 a.m.	*deśākṣi* and *bilahari*
10 a.m.	*sāveri, dhanyāśi, bhairavi*
3 to 4 p.m.	*pūrvi kalyāṇi*
6 p.m.	*śaṅkarābharaṇam, kalyāṇi, nāṭṭa*
8 p.m.	*toḍi, kāmbhoji, yadukulakāmbhoji, nīlāmbari, mukhāri, ānanda bhairavi, kānakkuruñji*

2. *Śīveli*. In many temples, the portable deity (*utsava vigraha*) is taken to circumambulate the temple three times at morning, noon and night. This is done to the accompaniment of many instruments like *cheṇṭa, kompu, kuḻal*, etc. In some temples like Tiruvilvamala (Trichur district) special importance is given to the

kuḻal and the playing of several *rāga*s can be heard according to the time of the day.

3. In some temples during *pūjā*s (done with the doors of the sanctum closed — *Naṭa Aṭachchu Pūjā*) the *kuḻal* is played. This is replaced by *nāgasvaram* in many places.
4. During temple festivals, there are some special occasions when *kuṟum kuḻal* is to be played. The ritual is known as *viḷakku āchāram*.

The deity is brought out from the sanctum and kept in a convenient spot. Then several instruments are played individually. This is an occasion for the artists to demonstrate their talents. First a tāyampaka is played on the *cheṇṭa*. Then a *keḷi* or *paṟṟu* is played on the *maddaḷam*, then a *paṟṟu* is rendered on the *kompu* and finally a *paṟṟu* is played on the *kuḻal*. Normally only one person plays. He is accompanied by a *śruti* (drone), a *cheṇṭa* and one *ilattāḷam* (big size cymbals). The playing is started with a few snatches of *nāṭṭa rāga*. Then the main *rāga* is elaborated. Usually *kāmbhoji, kalyāṇi, śaṅkarābharaṇam, bhairavi, ānanda bhairavi, nīlāmbari, mukhāri, devagāndhāri*, etc. are played. Then the rendering of the *paṟṟu* proper starts. This is akin to the rendering of a *pallavī*. The rhythm keepers join only at this stage, unlike the *nāgasvaram* where the *tavil* is played even during the short intervals of the playing of the *rāga*. First it is rendered in *viḷamba kālam*. Then it is rendered in faster tempo when usually another *rāga* will be played. The *tāḷa* used is normally only *chempaṭa* (*ādi tāḷa*). After rendering in the faster tempo, a *naṭa* is played, usually *tiśram*. This is called *kūṟu vāyikkal*. Then *suruṭṭi rāga* is played in a *tāḷa* of 4 *mātrā*s (three beats and a wave). Then a *kalāśam* (*muttāyippu*) is played in *eka tāḷa* and *madhyamāvati rāga*. For this sometimes only one cymbal is used by beating it with a stick (a miniature *Ceṅgila* or *chembakālam*). If time permits some *kīrtanas* are rendered before doing the final *muttāyippu* in *eka tāḷa*. For this the *ku<u>l</u>al* is accompanied on a *toppi maddaḷam* and not by *cheṇṭa*.

It is a pity that a real top-class *pa<u>rr</u>u* is no longer available to be enjoyed. The *pa<u>rr</u>u* playing in Tripunithura temple in its hey-day used to take about 4 hours on Valiaviḷakku festival day. This should give an idea of the importance given to *ku<u>l</u>al*.

The next function in the festival is known as the *iṭakka pradakṣiṇam*. The deity is taken round the temple to the accompaniment of instruments like *iṭakka, toppi maddaḷam, kompu, timila* and *ku<u>l</u>al*. In some temples importance is attached to the playing of *ku<u>l</u>al* during this procession. First *nāṭṭa rāga* is played. Some *rakti rāgas* are rendered set normally to *tripuṭa* (or *miśra chāppu*) *tāḷam*. The *rāgas* heard normally are *yadukulakāmbhoji, pāṭi, ānanda bhairavi, kānakkurīñji*, etc. Some *padams* are also played. One such is *māttāḍa ba<u>r</u>a dēnō*. Some of the *śṛṅgāra padams* of Kathakali may also be used. In areas surrounding Tiruvilvamala temple a *padam* heard is *Kāminī Maṇi*. On probing into the matter I was delighted to find that this is a *Maṇi Pravāḷa pada* of Swati Tirunal. The full text is given below. The subject matter of the same is a conversation between a *nāyikā* and her *sakhī*. The *nāyikā* asks, "why is perspiration seen on your face, why are your eyes red, why is your hair dishevelled," etc. The *sakhī* gives evasive replies and finally the *nāyikā* concludes that they are proof that her maid through whom she had sent a message to her Lord had herself had a union with Lord Padmanābha.

It may be mentioned here that some of the court musicians of Trivandrum were natives of Tiruvilvamala and the last remnants of the original Mohinī Āṭṭam survived at the same place. Thanks to poet Vallathol this was revived at the Kerala Kalamandalam. The song *Kāminī Maṇi* was one of the songs used for Mohini Āṭṭam long ago. The original *rāga* seen for this song is a strange one — *pūrva kāmodari* (or *pūrvikāmboji*). It is now rendered as a *rāgamālika*, usually in the *rāgas*, *pāṭi* (Kathakali type), *kānakkurīñji*, *punnāgavarāḷi*, and *gopikāvasantam*. The use of *tiśrajati tripuṭa*, the use of *rakti rāga*s and the use of some of the *śṛṅgāra pada*s during *iṭakka pradakṣiṇam* would go to show that at one time there might have been the dancing of women preceding the deity.[13]

---

13. *Śloka* 230, chapter 9 of *Tantrasamuccaya* (an authoritative treatise on temple rituals in Kerala) lends support to this point:

    śaṅkhapreṅkhaccaṭulapaṭahottāḷatāḷorubherī
    raṅgacchṛṅgoḍḍamaraḍamarūddīpravīṇā pravīṇāḥ
    ḍhakkāḍūkkāviraḷamuraḷīkarmaṭhāścābhiyāyuḥ
    sphāyaddīpāstamiha mahitoddā mahelā mahelāḥ

    A portion of the commentary on the *śloka* clarifies it as

    vilāsayuktāḥ prauḍhā yuvatyaḥ agre gaccheyuḥ

    i.e. the deity is preceded by young women of status and maturity in their lovely feminine gait.

    It is to be noted that *kuḻal* is not mentioned in the *śloka* though it mentions a number of other instruments. However *muraḷī* is mentioned though there is no tradition for the using of flute in temple worship in Kerala. It is therefore to be inferred that for want of a better equivalent in Sanskrit the word *muraḷī* has been used in the general sense of *suṣira vādya*.

After *iṭakka pradakṣiṇam, cheṇṭa meḷam* for the elephant procession starts. The procession is a slow one and they stay at some spots for a long time to complete one of the stages in *cheṇṭa*-playing. A *cheṇṭa meḷam* consists of a number of *cheṇṭas, ilattāḷams, kompus* and *kuḻals*. A few *cheṇṭas* will be rendering the *Vinyāsams* (complicated rhythms) while the rest of the *cheṇṭas* will be beating the time. There may be as many *kompus* and *kuḻals* as the number of *uruṭṭu cheṇṭas* (*vinyāsam* players). The *kuḻal* artists will be facing these *cheṇṭa* players and they effectively control the pace and *tāḷa* of the *cheṇṭa meḷam*. The chief of the *kuḻal* players will be showing signals by drawing circles in the air with his instrument (called *kuḻal minnikkuka*) to regulate the play and to show where the *kalāśams* (*muṭṭāyippu*) are to be played. During the interval between periodic *eṭa kalāśams* the *kuḻal* player may be playing some melody.

For example, for *pañchāri meḷam* in *cheṇṭa* the *tāḷa* is *rūpaka* of 6 *mātrās*. The first phase is done in an extremely slow tempo of 16 *kaḷā chaukkam* or 96 *mātrās*. The *eṭa kālam* will start at the 80th *mātrā*, from when on, the *kuḻal* also will play the *jātis* and continue it till the 16th *mātrā* of the next *tāḷavaṭṭam*. By his signs the *kuḻal* player will indicate the number of *mātrās* played.

There used to be some convention as to the *rāgas* to be played by the *kuḻal* artists for various *meḷams*, i.e. for the Cheṇṭa Meḷam rendered in different *tāḷams*. For pāṇṭi Meḷam, *bhairavi* is usually rendered in different *tāḷams*, for Pañchāri Meḷam, *śaṅkarābharaṇam; ārabhi* for *Chempaṭa* and *sāveri* for *chempa*, etc.

Unfortunately however at the present day no two *kuḻals* will have the same *śruti* and no two players will be rendering in the same way with the result that it will be a veritable cacophony, but during the *kalāśams* they will be playing the Jatis of the *tāḷam* and it would add to the over-all grandeur of the Cheṇṭa Meḷam. Thus during some stage of the Cheṇṭa Meḷam the *kuṟum kuḻal* has the function of only a *tāla vādya.*[14]

Kuṟum kuḻal is one of the instruments used in Kūṭiyāṭṭam, the traditional Sanskrit stage of Kerala. This theatre form as it exists today is considered to be more than a 1000 years old, its present form being shaped by the Chera King Kulaśekhara Varmā. The Chākyārs who do *abhinaya* in Kūṭiyāṭṭam are said to be the same community as the Chakkaiyan mentioned in *Śilappadikāram. Kuḻal* also is mentioned in *Śilappadikāram* as being used for the dances.[15] So this tradition of using the *kuḻal* in dance forms is nearly 2000 years old.

Unfortunately however at present there is no proper function for the *kuḻal* in Kūṭiyāṭṭam. The Sanskrit verses are only chanted and not sung. The *kuḻal* player renders

---

14. Even during a regular *kachcheri* in Carnatic Music when the vocalist renders *neraval* or *svaram* in quick tempo the violinist does not follow the artist in the usual way. He plays only *sa sa sa sa* and adds only to the *tāḷa*-effect and the violin acts as a *tāḷa* instrument for that brief period.

15. From the text of *Śilappadikāram,* it is not clear what the instrument Kuḻal is. The commentaries on the word *kuḻal* give details of the placement of holes which is like that of the flute. However the commentary also mentions that metal, wood or bamboo may be used for the instrument. In view of the fact that even primitive tribes are having *madhukarī* type instruments for dances we may take it that the *kuḻal* of *Śilappadikāram* may well be the *kuṟum kuḻal* type of instrument.

whatever *rāga* he feels is suitable for the occasion and in many cases it becomes a distraction to the enjoyment of the wonderful abhinaya of the Chākyārs.[16]

It is a tribute to the catholic outlook of the Music Academy, Madras that they at least evince interest in this art of Kerala which is now on its last legs.

Appendix

Kāminī Maṇi

A *pada* of Swati Tirunal Maharaja used for Mohini Āṭṭam and for rendering in *kuṟum kuḻal* in temples.

pūrva kāmodari Rāgam Aṭanta Tāḷam

(*pūrva kāmboji*) (Khaṇḍajāti Aṭa Tāḷam)

Nāyikā: *kāminī maṇi sakhi tāvaka mukhaminnu*
kāmam svinnamāyatentē vada?

Sakhī: *tāmarasabāndhava kiraṇameṟṟu vadanam*
tāntamāyi nitāmtam

Nāyikā: *tarunamṛganayanē tava locanayugaḷa-*
maruṇataramāyatentē hanta?

Sakhī: *taruṇī tava dayitavacanodita*
kopena paramāruṇamāyinnu

Nāyikā: *nīlanīradanibhamākum tava kuntaḷam*
bālē, luḷitamāyatentē? nava

Sakhī: *malayamārutacalanamatukoṇṭatrē*
cālē luḷitamāyinnu

Nāyikā: *kumkumapankamaḻivānentu kāraṇam*
kokilavāṇi tava kēḷkka?

---

16. See L.S. Rajagopalan, "Music in Kootiyattam", *Sangeet Natak*, 10, pp. 12-25 (1968).

Sakhī: *paṅkajākṣi sāmpratamuttarīya*
karṣaṇāl paricōṭaḻiññitaho

Nāyikā: *mēni vāṭuvānentumūlamennu paṛaka?*

Sakhī: *yānāyānattālatre bata*

Nāyikā: *māninī nīconnatellām satyam*
iniyum mama vācam śṛṇu kimapi
sarasanām śrī padmanābhanoṭu saha
sambhōgamatilenniyē ippoḷ
varatanu tavādharakṣatamāyateṅṅane
nirupamādhbhutatarāmgī?

(I am indebted to Dr. S. Venkitasubramonya Iyer, Prof. of Sanskrit, Trivandrum, for furnishing the correct text of the song quoted above.) The *ārohaṇa* and *avarohaṇa* of *pūrva kāmodari* (*pūrva kāmboji*) has not been traced. Aṭanta Tāḷa is Khaṇḍajāti Aṭa Tāḷa. The text of the song is a regular paraphrase of a *śloka* in *Amaruśataka* (*śloka* 118, Nirnayasagara edition):

khinnaṁ kena mukhaṁ divākarakaraiste rāgiṇī locane
roṣāttadvacanoditādvilulitā nīlālakā vāyunā
bhraṣṭaṁ kuṅkumamuttarīyakaṣaṇātklāntāsi gatyāgatair-
yuktaṁ tatsakalaṁ kimatra vada he duti! kṣatasyādhare

This may be translated as follows:

Lady: Why is perspiration on your face?

Maid: Due to sun's rays.

Lady: Why are your eyes red?

Maid: Due to his (your lover's) harsh words.

Lady: Why is your hair dishevelled?

Maid: Due to wind.

Lady : The *kumkum* (on your forehead) is lost.

The earliest reference to an instrument made of horn seems to be in the *Mahābhārata*[2] where it is referred to as *goviṣāṇikā* (made out of the horn of cow).

The reference in *Bhāgavata*[3] is more appropriate to our subject. The divine cowherd Kṛṣṇa is said to be having a *śṛṅga vādya* with him always in addition to the flute. One epithet of His is Śṛṅgapriya. Once when he wanted to set out for *vanabhojana* (a picnic in the forest) he roused his cow-herd friends early morning by blowing his *śṛṅga*.

In the Tamil classic *Śilappadikāram*, though the instrument is not mentioned in the text, the commentator Adiyārkunallār mentions that *kompu vādyam* was popular at that time.

The Malayālam poet Tuncattu Eḻuttacchan (sixteenth century CE) in his *Mahābhāratam Kiḷippāṭṭu* mentions *śṛṅga* along with several other instruments as being used in the Mahābhārata war.

Musical instruments made from animal horns are still used by tribal folks in India.[4] The instruments are known as *siṅgha, siṅghī, kōhuk*, etc. in north India. The Todas and Kotas[5] of Nilgiris use musical instruments made out of

---

2. *Mahābhārata*, Bhīṣma Parva, 43.8

   tato bheryaśca peśyaśca krakacā goviṣāṇikāḥ ।
   sahasaivābhyahanyanta tataḥ śabdo mahān abhūt ।।

3. *Bhāgavata*, 10th Skandha, 12th Adhyāya, 1st *śloka*

   kvacit vanāśāya mano dadhadvrajāt
   prātaḥ samuttāya vayasyavatsapān
   prabodhayan śṛṅgaraveṇa cāruṇā
   vinirgato vatsapurassaro hariḥ

4, 5, See Kothari, *Folk Musical Instruments of India*, New Delhi: Sangeet Natak Akademi.

commemoration of a victory of the Mahārājā of Cochin. Though the *mahārājā*s have become commoners, the procession continues as a people's procession.

Unlike other *suṣira vādyas*, there are no holes or stops for producing various notes in this instrument. It is used as a *laya vādya* in Kerala. The Keralite has a special aptitude for *laya* and he has raised this instrument from its primitive levels to that of a classical instrument for *laya*. Much of the attraction for *pañchavādyam* and *cheṇṭa meḷam* is due to the use of this instrument. It is essentially an outdoor instrument and its sound can be heard for miles around, especially in the villages.

Methods of Teaching

First the student is taught to make proper sounds with the *kompu*. The lips have to be rounded and the blowing proper. Normal blowing will give the basic note (*sa*) and harder blowing will give its higher octave. By controlled blowing it is possible to get *pa* and even its octave (*tāra pañchama*) but it requires much practice and strength of blow, else it is likely to produce discordant notes. Normal playing is therefore confined to the basic note and its higher octave. The strength of blow can vary the basic note by about a *śruti* (and naturally the higher octave also) and tonal variations are possible.

The student is then taught to play graded *jāti*s in *chempaṭa tāḷa* (*jhompaṭa* of *ādi tāḷa*). This *tāḷa* of 8 *mātrā*s is marked time by 3 beats and 1 wave and again 3 beats and 1 wave.

The mnemonics for the first lesson are *they, tha tha, thai, tha tha, they, tha tha, thai, dhey dhey.*

Formerly only the *timiri* instruments[11] were being used in temples. The *bāri* instrument is comparatively of recent origin. It came into prominence with the development and refinement of *pañchavādyam* by Venkichan Swamy. Of late *bāri* instrument is mainly used; the *timiri* is found more with Harijans who use it for their folk festivals.

In central Kerala area (former Cochin State and adjacent areas) only the Nair community plays this instrument in temples, whereas drums like *timila* and *cheṇṭa* were the almost exclusive preserves of the Mārār community. Notable exceptions are some Nampūtiri and Tamil brāhmins who became famous in playing some of these instruments. In all old and important temples, *kompu* is an essential instrument for daily *pūjā*, *Śīveli*, etc. During *utsavas* this instrument is used in all the temples. It is used as part of the ensemble for *Śrī Bhūta Bali*, *Vilakku-Āchāram*, *Kompu Pāṭṭu*, *Cheṇṭa Meḷam*, *Iṭakka Pradakṣiṇam* and *Pañchavādyam*. In folk religious festivals like Veṭṭakkorumakan Pāṭṭu, *Pāna*, *Teyyam*, *Muṭiyeṟṟu* etc. this instrument is used. Even the Harijans use this instrument for some of their festivals and dance. The Syrian Christians of Kerala use this instrument for some of their processions but the playing is done by Harijans usually. *Kompu* was one of the instruments used during the marching of armies in Kerala. Its martial tradition is still maintained in its use in the *Attachchamayam* procession in Tripunithura near Cochin. *Attachchamayam* procession was started in

11. Note the parallel in the temples of Tamil Nadu where only the shorter and high pitched *nāgasvaram* also called *timiri* was being used. The longer and lower pitched instrument (also called *bāri*) has come into prominence only recently.

4

Kompu Vādyam

KOMPU *vādyam* of Kerala belongs to the class of *suṣira vādyas* or wind instruments. Unlike other wind instruments this is not used for melody but only as a *laya* or *tāḷa* instrument. The word *kompu*[1] (in Malayalam and Tamil) literally means a horn. It is well known that horns of animals (especially cattle) were used as a primitive musical instrument in early times. In course of time, animal horn was replaced by metal and the shape also underwent many changes. The Sanskrit word for *kompu* is *śṛṅga* and the instrument is mentioned with that name in the Purāṇas.

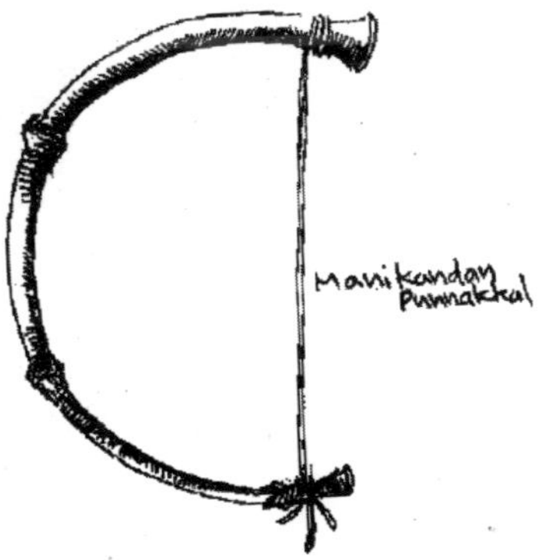

Kompu

1. "A Draviḍian Etymological Dictionary" by Burrow and Emeneau says that the word is of pure Draviḍian origin and is used in Tamil, Malayalam, Canarese and Tulu.

Maid: It was brushed off by the upper garment.

Lady: You are tired.

Maid: Due to going and coming.

Lady: Well, all that is proper; but then tell me my maid,
How has your lower lip cut?

Swati Tirunal has only added one line that the Maid must have had union with Lord Padmanābha, a twist that elevates the episode to a spiritual plane. The *sambodhana*s used by the Lady and the Maid added by Swati Tirunal also add to the beauty of the dancing.

Demonstrations: Kuḻal — Manathanath Narayanan Nair of Tiruvilvamala, and Cheṇṭa — Annamanada Parameswara Marar.

Nine different variations of this pattern are taught.

The second lesson is the playing of different *jāti*s for 4 *tāḷavaṭṭams*.

Third lesson is the *kalaśam* (*muttāyippu* or *moṟa*).

After these preliminary lessons the student is initiated into the playing of *kompu* for *Cheṇṭa Meḷam*.

Cheṇṭa Meḷam is an ensemble of a large number of *cheṇṭa* (drums). The other instruments which join the *meḷam* are *ilattāḷam* (Brahma *tāḷam*), *kuḻal* (similar to *timiri nāgasvaram*) and *kompu*. Among the *cheṇṭa* artists a good number will beat out the *tāḷa* on the booming (*valam tala*) side of the *cheṇṭa*.

There will be a number of *kompus*. They play together for every *kalāśam* which is played at the end of every few *tāḷavaṭṭams*. Before the start of the *kalāśam* all the *kompus* will get ready by blowing the lower note. The people on top of the elephants holding the *ālavaṭṭam* (peacock-feather fan) and *veñchāmaram* (yak tail swish) will take their cue and stand up holding their fan and swish ready. When the *kalāśam* is played the swish is waived. This is one of the most picturesque sights of the elephant procession in Kerala.

The *kompu* will play for one more *tāḷavaṭṭam* after the *kalāśam*.

For *Cheṇṭa Meḷam*, different *tāḷa*s are used. The *kompu* artist has to be proficient in all these *tāḷa*s. Normally *Cheṇṭa Meḷam* is played in *pañchāri* (*rūpakam*), *pāṇṭi* (*tiśrajāti tripuṭa*) and *chempaṭa* (*ādi*).

The following *tāḷa*s are also used:

Aṭanta (*khaṇḍa jāti aṭa*)

Chempa (*miśra jāti jhampa*)

Dhruva (*chaturaśra jāti dhruva*)

Añchaṭanta tāḷa (a *tāḷa* of 16 *mātrās*)

For *aṭanta tāḷa* the time is kept by showing 4 beats 1 wave, 4 beats 1 wave, one beat one wave, one beat one wave (total 14 *mātrās*).

Añchaṭanta tāḷa which seems to be peculiar to Kerala is kept by 5 beats 1 wave, 5 beats 1 wave, 1 beat 1 wave, 1 beat 1 wave (total 16 *mātrās*). The name is probably derived because instead of four beats of *aṭanta tāḷa*, 5 beats are made for *añchaṭanta* (*añchu* means five). This *tāḷa* does not fit in the *sapta tāḷa* scheme or 108 *tāḷa* scheme of Carnatic Music.

Laya-vinyāsa on the *kompu* is known as *kompu pa̲r̲r̲u*. During temple festivals before the idol (*utsava vigraha*) is taken round the temple on elephants (*pradakṣiṇā*), the idol is brought to the outer courtyard of the temple and kept on view. Individual instruments like *kompu, ku̲ḻal, maddaḷam*, etc. are brought in front of the idol and they are played one after another. Such demonstrations on the instruments are called *pa̲r̲r̲u vayikkuka*.

The duration of the playing of *kompu* may be up to an hour depending on the ability of the artist and the time available. *Pa̲r̲r̲u* is usually played in *chempaṭa, aṭanta, añchaṭanta, chempa* or *tala tericca chempa*. *Tala tericca chempa* is a picturesque colloquial name given by these artists for *khaṇḍa jāti tripuṭa ṭāḷa* of nine *mātrās*. Since it is one *mātrā* short of *chempa tāḷa* of 10 *mātrās*, they call it *chempa* with its end cut-off (*tala tericca* — end cut-off).

Kompu is one of the main instruments in *pañchavādyam* of Kerala. Here also as in *Cheṇṭa Meḷam*, the *kompu* is played mainly during the *Kalāśams* of the *pañchavādyam*. At this juncture *ālavaṭṭam* and *veñchāmaram* will be exhibited on top of the elephants.

The artist here Sri Kandangi Appu Nair of Machat is attached to the Bhagavatī Temple of Thiruvanikkavu of Machat near Vadakkancheri of Trichur district. In this temple some extra importance is given to *kompu vādyam*. During the annual *Pa<u>r</u>a* ceremony, paddy offerings are collected from people miles around. Only one *ku<u>l</u>al* and four *kompus* are used. No drums are played. As a lot of distance and houses have to be covered, the temple servants have to run literally — the *kompu* players as well.

At the temple at Maruthoor near Guruvayoor a very big sized *kompu* is used but of late only the last piece of it is used just to sound it like a conch during *dīpārādhana*.

The instrument *kompu* is developed in a purely Indian tradition and with its martial traditions as mentioned earlier, is well suited for use in the Army in place of the bugle for sounding Revielle, Retreat, etc. Will the Indian Army adopt it?

5

Cheṇṭa

THE *laya-vinyāsa* done on the *cheṇṭa* in Kerala is known as *tāyampaka*. The origin of the word *tāyampaka* is obscure. Some people explain it as *tāḷam vaka,* i.e. varieties of *tāḷa* played on the instrument or as *tāḷam paka,* i.e., a fight with the *tāḷas*. However the explanation of Sri Attoor Krishna Pisharoti seems to be the most appropriate. He says it is derived from *sthāyam vaka,* that is varieties of *sthāya*. In the *Saṅgīta Ratnākara, sthāya* is defined as *rāgasya avayavaḥ sthāyaḥ*. *Sthāya* means *saṅgatis*. So the playing of various *saṅgatis* on the *cheṇṭa* becomes *sthāyam vaka* which later became *tāyampaka*.

The name *cheṇṭa* is probably derived from the sound it makes: *jham ḍa*. The *cheṇṭa* is a tall hollow cylinder covered

Ceṇṭa

on both sides with cow hide. The old specifications for the cylinders is from the word *maram* which in *ka-ṭa-pa-yādi* will be the figure 25 which is the length plus diameter (about 16½ viral long and 7¼ viral diameter). The thickness of the wood is to be 4 to 6 *tora*s.

8 toras — 1 viral (two finger spans)

24 viral — 28 inches

The cylinder is usually of jack wood. A bamboo piece heated and bent into a circle and covered with leather is used as a ring at the top and the bottom to hold the leather. Cow hide is used to cover the faces on each side. At the edge one piece of leather is added on for tying the tension strings. 12 holes are made and the strings (made of *vakka* fibre) are passed through and tightened by movable tightening loops holding adjacent strings. The left end has only one piece of leather but in the right end seven additional circular pieces of diminishing diameters are pasted on with a special gum on the inside. The pasting of these pieces gives it a booming sound. This right end is played only for tāntric worship, when "gods" are brought on the stage in Kathakali, for keeping time when playing *tāyampaka*, etc. Nowadays *cheṇṭa* can be seen having metal fastening for keeping the tension.

When the *tāyampaka* is played the strings are tightened to give a higher *śruti* and while playing the *meḷam*s in elephant procession a lower tension is given. The instrument can produce about 7 tones when playing with the hand (left hand) *dhum* and *dhom* according to whether the striking is with the flat palm or with the edge of the palm. *Ta* and *dhi* sounds are heard similarly when the *cheṇṭa* is sounded at the edge.

If a stick (in the right hand) is used, *du* and *nnam* sounds are heard when the middle and the edge are struck. When the portion in between the edge and the centre is struck the tone will be slightly different. More tonal effects, especially in Kathakali, are made by rubbing the leather with the stick or altering the tension on the leather with one hand while playing with the other. No fingering however is done when playing the *cheṇṭa*.

Tāyampaka is usually done at night only. After *dīpārādhana*, etc. in the evening the deity is brought out and kept in a *maṇḍapa* and *tāyampaka* is played as an offering. Before starting the actual *tāyampaka* a piece known as *sandhi vela* is rendered on the right end of the *cheṇṭa* in *eka tāḷa*. At the finish of *sandhi vela* playing (usually done by some assistants) the leader starts the *tāyampaka*. The *tāyampaka* is done only in *chempaṭa tāḷa* which is equal to the *ādi tāḷa* of Carnatic Music.

One man (the leader) plays the *vinyāsa* using his left palm and a stick in the right hand. There will be two *cheṇṭas* keeping time beating on the left or tension end. Two more will be keeping time beating on the right end. Two or three cymbals will also be keeping time.

The playing lasts 1 to 1½ hours. It is in 5 stages: *pati kālam, kūṟu, iṭavaṭṭam, iṭanila,* and *irikiṭa*.

Pati kālam is slow tempo. The *tāḷa* beats are done as

1	2	3	4	5	6	7	8
nnam	*nnam*	*nnam*	*dhim*	*nnam*	*dhim*	*nnam*	*dhim*

The *pati kālam* is in *chaturaśra naṭa* and it is played in three or four increasing tempos. However the tempo is not on the pattern of *viḷamba, madhyama* and *druta tāḷa* of

Carnatic Music. They slowly increase the tempo as in the pattern of singing *nāmāvalis* in *bhajana*. *Pati kālam* is played for about half an hour. Then *kūṟu* is played. *Kūṟu* playing is only playing of different *naṭas*, *tiśram* (*pañchāri kūṟu*), *khaṇḍam* (*chempa kūṟu*), *miśram* (*aṭanta kūṟu*). It is to be noted that *pañchāri tāḷa* is *rūpaka tāḷa* of 6 *mātrās*, *chempa tāḷa* is *jhampa tāḷa* of 10 *mātrās* and *aṭanta tāḷa* is *aṭa tāḷa* of 14 *mātrās*.

When *chempa kūṟu* and *aṭanta kūṟu* are played the mode of keeping time is changed though the basic *chempaṭa tāḷa* is maintained.

This change of mode of time keeping will make it appear that the playing is on a different *tāḷa* though actually only a different *naṭa* is played. This is another difference in the Kerala system of playing *laya-vinyāsa*, from the Carnatic system.

For *chempa kūṟu* the *tāḷa* is as follows:

1	2	3	4
nnam nnam nnam	*nnam nnam nnam*	*nnam nnam nnam*	*nnam nnam dhim*
5	6	7	8
nnam nnam nnam	*nnam nnam dhim*	*nnam nnam dhim*	*nnam dhi dhi dhim*

For *aṭanta kūṟu*, the *tāḷa* is kept as follows:

1	2	3	4
nnam nnam	*nnam*	*nnam nnam*	*dhim*
5	6	7	8
nnam nnam	*dhim*	*dhi dhi*	*dhim*

Kūṟu playing lasts about twenty minutes. This is also done in increasing tempos.

The *iṭavaṭṭam* is played for about five minutes. The *tāḷa* is kept:

dhim nnam dhim nnam dhim nnam, etc., etc.

Then the *iṭanila* is played, the time keeping being done as

dhim *dhim* *dhim*

After about ten minutes of this, the last very fast tempo *irikiṭa* is played for ten minutes.

As already mentioned, the peculiarities of the Kerala system of *laya-vinyāsa* is that the tempo of playing is slowly increased. The time keeping *cheṇṭa* must also automatically increase the tempo of their time keeping accordingly. While different *naṭa*s are played a different mode of time keeping is adopted suitable to the *naṭa*.

The *vinyāsa* is done only in *chempaṭa* or *ādi tāḷa*.

While with a bit of practice, it should be possible to do *laya-vinyāsa* on other *tāḷa*s also, it is not known why it is not done. It should however be mentioned that in Kathakali, before the start of the play, there is a *meḷa pada* in which the *cheṇṭa* and the *maddaḷam* do *laya-vinyāsa* in *jhampa tāḷa* (*jhampa* of 10 *mātrā*s).

Tāyampaka can be played on other instruments also. It is done on a wooden bow which is popular.

Laya-vinyāsa on the *maddaḷam* is known as *maddaḷa paṟṟu* and that on the *kompu* is *kompu paṟṟu*. Though they are also delightful to hear they are not elaborated like the *tāyampaka* on the *cheṇṭa*. *Tāyampaka* can be heard during most temple festivals.

Tāyampaka is taught by first reciting the *vāyttāri* (*chol-keṭṭu*). Young persons are given regular training for playing it.* Once this is learnt, they learn the playing of other *meḷams*,

* The trainee first practices certain set pieces by beating on a rock or wooden piece with a thick heavy stick in the hand. →

etc. Some special techniques are required in playing *cheṇṭa* in Kathakali and this is taught separately but the first lessons are *tāyampaka*.

Of late, some innovations like giving some special sound effects are done in *tāyampaka* but this is looked upon with disfavour by the older generation.

This *laya-vinyāsa* of Kerala has a definite message for connoisseurs outside the region and it augurs well for the art that an august body like this Music Academy is taking interest in it.

Tāyampaka (*Laya-Vinyāsa*) on the *Cheṇṭa*
by
Sri Trittala Kesava Poduval and party

Demonstration on the *iṭakka* and *sōpāna* Music by
Sri Tiruvegapura Rama Poduval
(Father of Sri Trittala Kesava Poduval)

Explanation by
Sri L.S. Rajagopalan of Trichur

Sri Rama Poduval is one of the few persons who know the various aspects of drumming for tāntric worship in Kerala temples. He is sponsoring the starting of a school for Kṣetra Kala in Kerala.

→ The practice with the heavy stick enables him to do the actual playing with the light stick on the drum daily.

In olden days there used to be a method of practice known as *Nilāvirikkal* (sitting in moonlight). After the new moon day the student is to practise for the duration of the moonlight. So from about an hour on the first day (*prathama*) the period of practise increases to 12 hours on full moon day and then it reduces daily to nil on the next new moon day.

6

Timila

TIMILA is one of the lively important drums used in Kerala. It is an elongated hour-glass shaped instrument. Its body is of jackwood. The length is about 2 ft and the diameter at the mouth 6 inches. The leather used is that of a cow calf fixed to a sort of cane rings and this covers the two ends. Twisted cow-hide straps are used as tension strings. The drum is suspended over the shoulders and the playing is done with both the bare palms. Playing is done only on one side. Only two tones are produced — *tha* and *thom* and so all *jāti*s have to be produced by the quick beat of the palms. Unlike as in the case of other instruments like the *mṛdaṅga,* both the hands have the same function and have to be equally adept; also individual fingers are not used.

Though *timila* is found mentioned even in the Tamil Classic *Śilappadikāram,* its use is now confined to Kerala. The word *timila,* according to some grammarians, is derived from the word *timi* (a fish). Its shape is said to resemble the

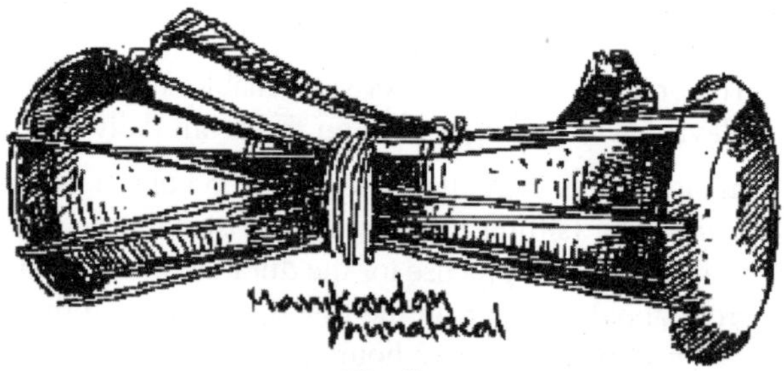

Timila

fish *timi*. Regarding the origin of the instrument there is an interesting mythological story.

The Asura Śūrapadma, devotee of Lord Śiva while witnessing the *Pradoṣa Sandhyā Tāṇḍava* (Dance) of Lord Śiva, expressed a desire to have Śiva's *ḍamarū* to keep *tāḷa* for the dance. Lord Śiva advised him to get an instrument made for himself. Śūrapadma in his haughtiness made a much bigger and longer instrument, but it would not give a proper sound. He again approached Lord Śiva who pointed out the absence of the hole in the middle of the instrument and the Lord with his own left finger drove a hole in the middle thus making an outlet for air in the hollow wooden piece.

When the skins were again fixed and played the sound was a perfect *oṁkāra*. Humbled but overjoyed Śūrapadma prostrated before the Lord shouting in ecstacy *mṛtyuñjaya hara hara śambho*. Lord Śiva was pleased and told him: Let the *tāḷa* of your chant be the *tāḷa* for playing the instrument and you can join Nandi (the Bull) who plays the *maddaḷam* for my dance. The *tāḷa* is *tripuṭa tāḷa* of 7 *mātrās*.

mṛ	*tyuñ*	*jaya*	*hara*	*hara*	*śam*	*bho*
tari	*kiṭa*	*ta*	*tari*	*kiṭa*	*taka*	*tom*
1	2	3	4	5	6	7

That is supposed to be the divine origin of the instrument and of the association of *maddaḷam* and *timila* for *pañchavādyam*.

The use of *timila* is primarily connected with temple rituals in Kerala. It is the most important instrument of the *pañchavādyam* ensemble. *Pañchavādyam* is an orchestra of

Tāḷa	*No. of Mātrās*	*Aṅgas*
Eka tāḷam	1	L
Śambhu tāḷam	2	DDG
Raṇṭām tāḷam	3	LG
Maṅgala tāḷam	4	GLL
Śakaṭu tāḷam	4	LLG
Muṭakku tāḷam	5	GLG
Takaṭṭu tāḷam	6	GGG
Mūnnām tāḷam	7	PGG
Nālām tāḷam	8	PLGG
Añchām tāḷam	9	PLLGG

tāḷa vādyas. There are two types of *pañchavādyam*: *kriyāṅga pañchavādyam* and *sevāṅga pañchavādyam*.

Kriyāṅga Pañchavādyam is connected with temple rituals known as *Śrībali* (*Śīveli*), *Śrī Bhūta Bali, Utsava Bali, Iṭakka Pradakṣiṇam*, etc. The following instruments are used: *pāṇi maram, iṭakka, cheṇṭa* (right hand end only), *timila, Ceṅgila* and *śaṅkha*. Different *tāḷa*s are prescribed for the various rituals. There are *tāḷa*s prescribed for the worship of *dikpāla*s, Brahmā and other deities of the Hindu pantheon. The following are some of the *tāḷa*s used. The symbols used for the *aṅga*s of the *tāḷa*s are *L = Laghu, G = Guru, P = Pluta, D = Druta*. It may be noted that different *tāḷa*s are used for the same purpose in different temples depending on whether a Vaiṣṇavite or Śaivite or Śākteya system is followed in the particular temple.

Some of the *tāḷa*s are used in very slow tempo, for which there is certainly a scientific basis, but it is not worthwhile discussing in detail from the general musical point of view.

That brings us to *sevāṅga pañchavādyam* and the use of

timila in the same. The instruments now used for this are *timila, maddaḷam, iṭakka, kompu, ilattāḷam* and *śaṅkha*. It is one of the most delightful combinations of *tāḷa vādyas* in Kerala. Unlike the *Cheṇṭa Meḷam* of Kerala where only a set mnemonics (*vāyttāri and cholkeṭṭu*) is used and where there is little scope for improvization in *pañchavādyam*, there is a lot of scope for individual improvisation especially for the *timila* and the *maddaḷam* artists. Hence *pañchavādyam* is deservedly considered to be on a superior level to *Cheṇṭa Meḷam*. It must however be mentioned that in the *tāyampaka*, on the *cheṇṭa* there is even greater scope for individual improvization but it is essentially the performance of a single artist and not that of a group like *pañchavādyam*.

It is only about 50 or 60 years since *pañchavādyam* was elevated to this higher artistic level. One Venkitachala Iyer (Venkichan Swami) of Tiruvilvamala and one Madhava Warrier were mainly responsible for effecting the reforms in the playing of *pañchavādyam*. It was they who brought about the present mode and order of playing the instruments in vogue. Formerly *maddaḷam* was being played on only one side like the *timila* (in vertical position). Due to their reform it is being played on both sides as at present (in horizontal position). *Pañchavādyam* is mainly used during temple processions and after *dīpārādhana* at sunset in temples during festival days. Of late it is being used even during receptions accorded to VIPs.

The *vādyam* is well developed only in the central areas of Kerala. A full set consists of 7 *timilas*, 4 *maddaḷams*, 9 *ilattāḷams*, 7 *kompus*, 1 *iṭakka* and 1 *śaṅkha*. At present an ensemble of 11 *timilas*, 5 *maddaḷams*, 11 *ilattāḷams*, 9 *kompus*, etc. are seen. Some of the best performances can be heard during the *Pooram* festival at Trichur. A performance may last from one to four hours, the tempo of playing being adjusted according to the availability of time.

Before considering the actual playing it may be worthwhile to consider the *tāḷa*s used in Kerala especially

Tāḷas	***Mātrās***	***Equivalent in Carnatic Music***
Chempaṭa	8	*Chaturaśra jāti tripuṭa*
Aṭanta	14	*Khaṇḍa jāti aṭa*
Muri aṭanta	7	*Tiśra jāti tripuṭa*
Chempa	10	*miśra jāti jhampa*
Pañchāri	6	*Chaturaśra jāti rūpaka*
Ekam	4	*Chaturaśra jāti eka*

in non-ritualistic or secular music. The *tāḷa*s used are identical with those in Carnatic music though they are called by different names.

However it should be noted that the concept of *jāti* (*tiśra, miśra*, etc.) for the *laghu aṅga*s of the *tāḷa*s as is found in Carnatic Music is absent in the *tāḷa*s of Kerala. When they keep time for the *tāḷa*s, the *aṅga*s will not be shown in the

Tīśra gati	*Pañchāri kūṟu*
Miśra gati	*Aṭanta kūṟu*
Khaṇḍa gati	*Chempa kūṟu*

normal way done in Carnatic Music. Normally *chaturaśra jāti* is used. However during elaboration (*vinyāysa*) different *gati*s are played. For *gati,* the term used is *kūṟu*.

The equivalent term for *sūladi tāḷa*s is *chuḻadi tāḷa*s. *Dhruva tāḷam* is seen used in *Cheṇṭa Meḷam* and in *miḻāvu* playing in Kūṭiyāṭṭam; *maṭhya tāḷam* is not seen but *muṭakku tāḷam* seems to be its equivalent. The *viḷamba, madhyama* and *druta kāla*s for the slow, medium and fast tempos are seen but in actual practice the speed is slowly increased as is done in *bhajana*s during the playing of each of the tempo. It should be mentioned to the credit of Kerala drummers that they are very adept in the handling of extremely slow tempos of 56 or 112 *mātrā*s; their *sarva laghu* concept is very well developed.

The playing of the *pañchavādyam* commences after the *śaṅkha* is blown three times, the first beat starting at the middle of the 3rd *śaṅkha* blow. The first tempo consists of 56 *mātrā*s, and though the *tāḷa* is supposed to be *tripuṭa* it is played in *chaturasra gati* as 7 × 8 *mātrā*s. This is called 7 *chempaṭa vaṭṭam*. Some set *jāti*s are played for some time and *vinyāsa*s are played on *maddaḷam, timila* and *iṭakka* individually. Then all the players join together for a *kūṭṭi koṭṭal* in set *jāti*s. The same sequence would be repeated at a slightly increased tempo according to the availability of time.

The second tempo of 28 *mātrā*s is not elaborated but played for a short time using a special *jāti* for the whole *tāḷa vaṭṭam* and the next stage of 14 *mātrā*s is taken up. The *tripuṭa* character of the *tāḷam* will be noticeable from now on. The next is 7 *mātrā*s and then a faster tempo of 3½ *mātrā*s. Finally they close it by playing *eka tāḷa*. *Timila* and *iṭakka* alone will be played in very fast tempo in the end and this is known as *timila eṭaccal* or *timila varakkal*.

There is a considerable scope for improving *pañchavādyam*. Only one *meḷam* in *tripuṭa tāḷa* is played at present. It is possible to introduce fresh *meḷam* in other *tāḷa*s.

The biggest handicap in the matter is the deplorable state of Temple finances, especially after the advent of Land Reforms in Kerala. As these are primarily temple-based, the patronage for them is steadily declining. Unless there is considerable effort by the government and the public these arts are likely to become extinct. Institutions like this Academy should give the right lead in preventing this catastrophe.

Demonstration by Annamanada Parameswara Marar and his student Sekharan

DEMONSTRATION (LEARNER'S LESSONS)

(1) *tha ki ta*

(2) *thaka tha ki ta*

(3) *tha ke tha ke tha ki ta*

(4) *tha ki ta thake*

(5) *kka tha ke thon ka thakre*

RITUALISTIC PORTION

1. Reciting the *vāyttāri* (mnemonics) and playing for *Utsava Bali* and the ritual at *mātṛkkallu.*
2. Reciting the *vāyttāri* and the playing for *Iṭakka Pradakṣiṇam.* (*Note*: It is this which is elaborated and sophisticated for the *pañchavādyam* for procession, etc.).

NON-RITUALISTIC PORTION

1. How the beats of *tāḷa* are shown and how the mnemonics are used for various *tāḷa*s in vogue in Kerala.
2. How *kūrū* (*gati* or *naṭa*) is played.
3. Regular *pañchavādyam* Portion

   The first tempo of 56 *mātrā*s was the equivalent of 8 *kaḷā chaukkam* of *tiśrajāti tripuṭa* but it is being played as 7 × 8 *chempaṭa* (*ādi tāḷa*) groups. But now this is again made still lower in tempo even as much as 1792 *mātrā*s. This slow tempo is only rarely played. Normally 896, 448, 224, 112 and 56 are played. For playing 1792 *mātrās* for one *chempaṭa vaṭṭa (ādi tāḷa)* it will be 256 *mātrās*. This portion will be demonstrated in mnemonics and played. It will take about 15 minutes for one full *tāḷavaṭṭa* of 1792 *mātrās*. Similar demonstrations for other stages and the quicker tempos of 28 *mātrās*, 14, 7 and 3 ½ will follow. The *vinyāsa* on the timila will conclude the demonstration.

Sri Parameswara Marar (age 62) who gave the demonstration belongs to an old family of temple drummers and hails from the village Annamanada in Trichur district. His family is attached to the Śiva Temple at Annamanada as hereditary drummers. Even as a young boy, he learnt to play *cheṇṭa, iṭakka* and other drums for temple rituals and processions.

He went to Kunnamkulam where his uncle was attached to a temple at Kakkad belonging to the Mankulam Princely family. There he learnt *maddaḷam* and *timila*. He was a *cheṇṭa* player for Kathakali when Kalamandalam was first started by the Manakkulam Raja at Ambalapuram in Trichur district. After 6 years of service he left the institution to work as free-lance *timila* player in *pañchavādyam*. Very soon he became chief *timila player* in several groups.

He has been *timila* instructor at Kerala Kalamandalam since 1965. He has trained several pupils including two Dutch gentlemen who had come to Kalamandalam (some years ago). He has also had some training in Carnatic Music.

He is currently engaged in writing a text book on *timila*, especially for *pañchavādyam* and the book is to be published by the Kalamandalam.

His student Sekharan is helping him in giving the demonstrations.

7

Mil̲āvu

THE *miḻāvu* is a percussion instrument of great antiquity. It has several unique features.

Shape

The shape of its body is something like an egg — the broader end up.[1] At the bottom end, there is a small hemispherical projection. The top has a cylindrical neck and the parchment is stretched over its mouth. A hole — the diameter of a pencil — is provided in the side of the body for proper resonance.

Use

The use of the *mil̲āvu* is exclusively for Kūṭṭu and Kūṭiyāṭṭam

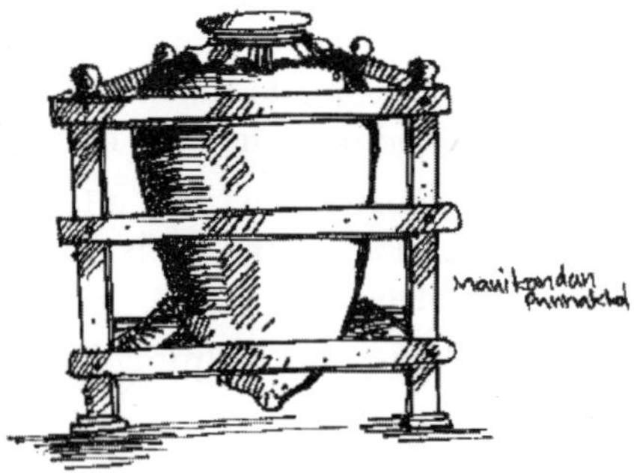

Mil̲āvu

1. Some people call the instrument erroneously as *pṭāv* since it resembles the big earthen vessel called Ptava used for storing paddy.

in Kerala temples. Kūṭṭu is a discourse on Purāṇas and Kūṭiyāṭṭam is an enactment of Sanskrit dramas. The *mil̲āvu* is not used for any other purpose. It is purely a "temple-based" instrument and is considered a *deva vādyam*.

Antiquity

Kūṭiyāṭṭam in Kerala has a tradition of more than a thousand years and the *mil̲āvu* has also at least that much tradition behind it. Moreover instruments by the name *mul̲a* and *moṭamul̲a* were in existence in Tamil Nadu for a long time and they were considered to be the same or similar instruments. References to *mul̲a* are found in *Śilappadikāram* during the description of dance, during the Indra festival, during the threshing of harvested paddy and as being used as an accompaniment for marching soldiers.[2] Another similar instrument, also in Tamil Nadu, is the *pañchamukha vādyam* which is a big pot-shaped instrument having five necks.[3] Parchments are stretched over these and the five faces give different tones.

The *Saṅgīta Ratnākara* of Śārṅgadeva mentions an instrument called *ghaṭa* in chapter 6 (Vādya Adhyāya):

ghanaḥ ślakṣṇaḥ supakvaśca stokavaktro mahodaraḥ ।
pāṇibhyāṁ vādyate tajjñaiścarmanaddhānano ghaṭaḥ ।।

It is a big bellied pot with its mouth covered by leather and played with both hands. The *Ratnākara* usually gives details of measurements, but it is silent about that aspect here. Hence we may consider the instrument as known but not popular at that time.

---

2. *Śilappadikāram*.
3. V. Raghavan, "The Multi-faced Drum", *Journal of the Madras Music Academy*, XXV, 1954, pp. 107-08.

Poets have compared the sound of the *miḻāvu* to thunder. The reverberation (*muḻakkam*) is referred to in Tamil literature.[4]

In China also there seems to be a counterpart to the *miḻāvu*.[5]

Material

Formerly, the *miḻāvu* used to be made of clay (*mṛt*). Hence in Kerala it is referred to as *mṛdaṅga* in Sanskrit — literally body being made of *mṛd* (clay).[6] Nowadays it is made of copper sheets. Instruments made of clay have a softer tone but the copper instruments are more resonant. Instruments made of clay are still in use in places like Panjal, Attur, in Trichur district and in Madayikkavu, Kurumathur in Cannanore district. There is a place called Miḻakunnu (also called Moḻakunnu) and as *mṛdaṅga śaila* in Sanskrit, where the temple of the *kuladevatā* (Śrī Porkali Bhagavatī) of the Rājā of Kottayam (Malabar) is located. The *miḻāvu* there is not only of clay, but is also considered to be *svayambhū* (self-manifested). The Rājā of Kottayam is famous as the author of Kottayam Kathakali plays. In the *vandana śloka*s to his plays he refers to the family deity as *mṛdaṅga śaila nilayāṁ*:

---

4. *Kaṇṇaśśa Rāmāyaṇa, Kiṣkindhā Kāṇḍa, Varṣa Varṇana* (b) *muḻāvin muḻakkam* as mentioned in Tamil Lexicon.
5. See K. Bharatha Iyer, *Kathakali*, p. 16.
6. *Nāṭyaśāstra*, chapter 33, p. 273 (Bibliotheca Indica edn.), *mṛdaṅga*s are called by that term because they are made of *mṛd*. But see V. Raghavan, *Journal of the Madras Music Academy*, XXIV, 1953, pp. 135-36, XXVI, 1955, p. 146 Why is *mṛdaṅga* so called?

durgāṁ cāpi mṛdaṅgaśailanilayām śrīporkalīmiṣṭadām ।
bhaktyā nityamupāsmahe sapadi naḥ kurvantvamī maṅgalam ॥

Rituals

In Kerala, Kūṭiyāṭṭam is considered a *chākṣuṣa yajña* — a visual sacrifice. Hence all important materials connected with this *yajña* have to be consecrated. The construction of the *kūttambalam* (temple theatre) is as much ritual-bound as the construction of the temple itself. Even the *chākyār* (the traditional actor) has to undergo a purificatory ceremony before he makes his debut as an actor. In a similar way the *miḻāvu* is also subjected to a long initiation ceremony.[7] The rituals for this are condensed in the following verse, in the book, *Śrī Kṛṣṇa Chintāmaṇi,* a book on Tantra by Sri K.P. Krishnan Bhattathiripad:

pīṭhe nyasya mṛdaṅgamiṣṭagaṇapo nāndyādipuṇyāhakṛt ।
tadbhūtāni viśodya nandicitimat snānāntavastrāvṛtam ॥

homo 'ṣṭadhruvasaṁskriyo yadi tadā dattopavītādikam ।
prācyārtoṣya ca rājayedgururatha prāvārako vādayet ॥

The *miḻāvu* is first kept on a ritual seating (over a *svastika* design, grains are spread and *darbha* grass kept on top). Gaṇeśa is first propitiated, then *puṇyāha*-water is sprinkled (consecration with holy water). *Nāndi* (pre-ritual prayers) is done, then *bhūta viśodhana* (symbolic purification of the five elements of the material of which the *miḻāvu* is made) is done and Nandikeśvara is invoked in it. Nandikeśvara is

7. *Nāṭyaśāstra* ch. 33, vv 259 to 284 deal with the installation ceremonies of drums. They are only a general worship. The ceremonies for the *miḻāvu* are quite different. It is a deification of the instrument.

offered symbolic bath and other item of welcome. The *miḻāvu* is draped with a cloth (dress offering). Then a *homa* is performed and eight of the sixteen *saṁskāras* (*garbhādhāna, puṁsavana, sīmantonnayana, jātakarma, nāmakaraṇa, annaprāśana, chauḷa* and *upanayana*) are performed. It is adorned with a sacred thread, black-buck skin and stick (of *palāśa* wood), etc. *Pūjā*, prayer, *naivedya*, etc. are done and then offering made with burning camphor, then the priest initiates the playing and then the Nambiar ties the skin and plays it.

Only members of the Nambiar community have the traditional right to play on the *miḻāvu*.[8]

The Nambiars are over-fond of playing the *miḻāvu*. Their ladies, the Naṅgyars are the traditional Cymbal players and play female roles in Kūṭiyāṭṭam. The Nambiars have to read the summary of plays known as Nambiar Tamil and they have to be proficient in music, dancing and instruments.

Directions for the ritual taken from tāntric manuscripts are given in the Appendix. The directions naturally are full of tāntric jargon and a knowledge of tāntric rituals is required to follow the directions properly. The whole idea is that Nandikeśvara is invoked to take his divine residence in the *miḻāvu* permanently. Nandikeśvara — in addition to being the *vāhana* of Śiva — is also the rhythm-keeper, *tāṇḍava*

---

8. There is a stanza recited by the *chākyār* apparently making fun of the Nambiars but which describes picturesquely the hereditary occupation (*Kula Toḻil*) of the Nambiars.

> *aṅgaṁ tanne mṛdaṅgamākki nitarām kaivilcakoṇṭuccakaiḥ* ।
> *rangaśrīyoṭu tāyamiṭṭu tuniyum naṅṅakuṭumbaṁ vahan* ॥
> *bhaṅgikkāi tamiḷ certa pustakavaram kaikoṇṭu kakṣāntare* ।
> *saṅgītārthamaho samāhitamatistan nambiār vannitu* ॥

tāḷikaḥ for Śiva's dance and hence it is that he is invoked in the instrument. The *mil̲āvu* has thus the status of a *parivāra devatā* of the temple. The *mil̲āvu* is therefore not taken outside the temple normally — if it be done, purificatory ceremonies will have to be performed.

If a *mil̲āvu* gets broken or becomes unusable, elaborate rituals are prescribed for its *saṁskāra* (burial). After purification and propitiation, the *chaitanya* of Nandikeśvara is transferred from the old *mil̲āvu* to a *kalaśa* (pot of holy water) and the water after necessary *pūjā*s and *homa*s is poured in the sanctum sanctoram to unite symbolically the *chaitanya* with the presiding deity. The broken *mil̲āvu* if of clay is buried after handing it over to Chaṇḍeśvara, the keeper of *Nirmālya.* If it be of copper, it is melted and re-used. The text of the ritual is not given here as it is pretty long.

Having the status of *parivāra devatā* of the temple, the size and dimensions of the *mil̲āvu* is governed by the principles of temple architecture and iconography. A search of all old tāntric manuscripts may reveal the directions regarding their size and dimensions though the attempts made by the author so far have not been able to locate them.

The size of the *mil̲āvu* made of copper at the *vadakkunnathan*, temple-theatre, Trichur is approximately 36 inches height, diameter at the widest point 26 inches. The neck protrudes about 5 inches from the main body and is about 6 inches in diameter.

The *mil̲āvu* is usually kept in a cage of wooden slats. Its bottom is not to touch the ground; the sides are therefore supported by reapers kept across the cage. It is kept in what is known as the *kūṭapasthāna* of the theatre — which is between the green room and the acting area (*nepathya* and *raṅgaśīrṣa*). This is evidently the best place from the point of view of acoustics. The *Nāṭyaśāstra* says that the drums should be arranged between the two doors of the green room.[9] This is correctly followed in the case of the *mil̠āvu*. Before the commencement of Kūṭiyāṭṭam the *mil̠āvu* is draped with a cloth as ordained in the *Nāṭyaśāstra*.[10]

Practise

Because of the divinity attached to it, the *mil̠āvu* is not played except for Kūṭṭu or Kūṭiyāṭṭam. A student therefore cannot practise on it and a separate practice instrument (*abhyāsa kur̠r̠i*) is made. This is a hollow cylinder of Jack or other suitable wood. A leather is stretched tight over one end face of this.

The beat is done with the open palm. Mainly two tones are produced — *tha* and *thu* — one by beating at the centre and the other near edge. Three or more learner's lessons are practised in four speeds.

1. *tha ki ta*
2. *dhi ka tha ka, dhi ka tha ka, dhi ka tha ka tha*
3. *tha ki ta kita tha ki thari kita kita thaki*

The *tāḷa*s used are:

---

9. *Nāṭyaśāstra*, ch. 14, v 2.

   ye nepathya gṛhadvāre mayā pūrvaṁ prakīrtite |
   tayorbhāṇḍasya vinyāso madhye kāryaḥ prayoktubhiḥ ||

10. *Nāṭyaśāstra*, ch. III, 3.74.

   ātoddhyāni tu sarvāṇi kṛtvā vastrottarāṇi tu

1. *Chempaṭa,* equivalent to *ādi tāḷa* (*jhompaṭa*) (8 *mātrā*s)
2. *Tripuṭa,* equivalent to *tiśra jāti tripuṭa* (7 *mātrā*s)
3. *Jhampa,* equivalent to *miśra jāti jhampa* (10 *mātrā*s)
4. *Dhruva,* equivalent to *chaturaśra jāti aṭa* (14 *mātrā*s)
5. *Aṭanta,* equivalent to *khaṇḍa jāti aṭa* (14 *mātrā*s)
6. *Eka Tāḷa,* equivalent to *chaturaśra jāti eka tāḷa* (4 *mātrā*s)

In addition one *tāḷa* of 20 *mātrā*s (double of *jhampa*) according to the *vāyttāri* (*cholkeṭṭu*) *mukkuṟṟī tiritāḷī pāṭai paṭalai paṛiccu koṇḍattu* is used. It is called Lakṣmī *tāḷa.*

Restrictions in the use of Tāḷas

Different *tāḷa*s are prescribed for use in Kūṭiyāṭṭam according to the situation, character (on the stage), type of gait, etc. Similar restrictions are also there on the use of the *svara* (the type of chant equivalent to a *rāga*) used. There are some verses with *chākyār*s on the use of these *tāḷa*s (and also on the *svaras*).[11]

1. *muḍḍārtta vīratarkeṣu ceṭīpañchama dāṇayoḥ* ।
   kurakkuruñjirāge ca dhruvatālaḥ prakīrtitaḥ ।।
2. *śrīkaṇṭhī toṇḍu puranīr kaiśikyāmindaḷe 'pi ca* ।
   ekatāḷo vinirdiṣṭo bhinnapañchamaduḥkhayoḥ ।।
3. *ghaṭṭantaryākhya rāge ca tarke cāntarisaṁjñike* ।
   tripuṭā tāḷa eva syāt saviḷambitamātrakaḥ ।।
4. *madhyamamātrāṁ tripuṭāṁ velādhūlyām vadanti tālajñāḥ* ।
   aparaiḥ punarapi nāṭye dhruva iti kaiścitddrutaḥ samākhyātaḥ ।।

11. Refer Author's article, "Music in Kootiyattam", *Sangeet Natak,* 10.

5. *śrīkāmare ca paurāḷyām tripuṭātidhrutā matā* ।
muralīndaḷa rāge tu dhruvatāḷo viḷambitaḥ ।।

6. *ekatāḷena kāryam syāt anyatsarvam yathocitam*

The names of the *svara*s (or *rāga*s) in the above verses are as follows: *muḍḍan, vīratarkan, cheṭipañchamam, dāṇam, kurakkuruñji, śrīkaṇṭhi, toṇḍu, puṟanīr, kaiśiki, indaḷam, ghaṭṭantari, tarkan, antari, velādhūli, śrīkāmaram, paurāḷi, muralīndaḷam.*

There are other verses which specify the situations where these *svara*s are to be used. Some of these names are reminiscent of the names of Tamil pans and others of *rāga*s not in vogue now.

The above verses may be summarized as follows after correlating them with the restriction on the use of *svara*s.

Tripuṭa tāḷa, medium tempo — used in *bhayānaka,* perplexed conditions, some dances like "beating the war drum," *yāśi yāśi pullarikka,* occasion of conveying (by shouting) a message to some one.

Tripuṭa tāḷa, slow tempo, in *krodha, raudra* in some dances like *jāti,* during the receiving of the news of the death of an evil character.

Tripuṭa tāḷa, fast tempo, in unexpected joy, in climax of love (*śṛṅgāra mūrchana*).

Dhruva tāḷa used in *adbhuta, bhayānaka, vīra* and *śṛṅgāra,* in some dances like *nitya kriyā valiya keśādipādam.*

Dhruva tāḷa, slow tempo in Śrī Rāma's *saṁbhoga śṛṅgāra.*

Dhruva tāḷa, fast tempo. For occasions not mentioned specifically elsewhere.

Eka tāḷa, used in *śānta, hāsya, bībhatsa* and *adbhuta*; at the end of an act, during the killing of an evil character, for describing the rainy season.

In addition, the following are used:

Aṭa tāḷa is used when a character acts that he hears what others are saying.

Chempaṭa tāḷa is used at the start of the play (*goṣṭhī*).

Jhampa tāḷa is used in certain dances and in some movements of Yaugandharāyaṇa.

Lakṣmī tāḷa is prescribed when the drummer does not know what exactly has to be used. It is equivalent to the playing of *sarva laghu* in Carnatic Music.

After studying the playing of the *tāḷa*s, the student has to learn to follow the acting of Kūṭiyāṭṭam. He has to familiarize himself with all the plays that are acted so that he can play the appropriate *tāḷa* in the proper tempo as the occasion demands. He has the disadvantage that he is sitting behind the actor and can see only his back.

The Kerala Kalamandalam offers a four-year course of *Mil̲āvu*. A few students have come out after training but the handicap is they cannot practise the art since Kūṭiyāṭṭam is performed only occasionally. Its uplift lies in the uplift of Kūṭiyāṭṭam itself.

Acknowledgements

Sri P.K. Narayanan Nambiar and Sri A. Madhava Chakyar of Irinjalakuda have supplied me with the *śloka*s on *tāḷa*s.

Sri K.P.C. Narayanan Bhattathiri of Perumanam and Sri Madhava Chakyar have supplied me with the details of the ritual.

Sri K. Divakaran Namboodiripad, chief Adhyāpaka of Tantra Vidyā Pīṭham, Chowannur has helped in understanding the rituals.

Sri. K.P. Narayana Pisharoti, Sri. N.K. Mukunda Pisharoti and Prof. S. Hariharan have helped with suggestions and reference books.

Note : Sri P.K. Narayanan Nambiar is preparing a text (1974) on the *miḻāvu* and it is expected to deal exhaustively on the subject, especially the practical side of playing on it.

Appendix

Mṛdaṅgopanaynaprakāraḥ

raṅge svastikam vā aṣṭadalam vā padmaṁ kṛtvā
brahmakalaśoktavat pīṭhaṁ
viracayya vitānādibhiralaṁkṛtya vistaraṁ saṁsthāpya
uttare cature chaturaśram kuṇḍaṁ kṛtvā
navāmbharadharaḥ sottarīyaḥ tatpaścime
ācāryaḥ samāsīnaḥ dehaśuddhi
śaṅkhapūraṇātmārādhanāḥ kṛtvā
gaṇeśaṁ saṁpūjya sthalaśuddhim kṛtvā,
śaivoktavat pīṭhaṁ saṁpūjya mūrtipaiḥ saha mṛdaṅgasya
puṇyāhaṁ kṛtvā,
mṛdaṅgasya bhūtasaṁhāraṁ kṛtvā,
kuṇḍasya paścime upaviśya
śaivoktavat aprijananaṁ kṛtvā
upaniṣkrāmaṇaṁ viṇā upanayanāntam aṣṭakriyāḥ kṛtvā,
śruveṇaiva kriyānte pṛthak pṛthak homamantreṇa saṁspṛśet
kuṇḍe mūrtikalpanāṁ kṛvtā, pakvaṁ hutvā,
caturdravyaṁ palāśaśamidādi hutvā,
sviṣṭakriyādi homaṁ samāpya tīrthaprokṣaṇāntaṁ
pūjāṁ kṛtvā mṛdaṅge nandinaṁ āvāhya aṅgāni

vinyasya snānāntaṁ upahāraṁ datvā
vastrasthāne vastreṇāveṣṭya dānaṁ muhūrtam ca kṛtvā
nīrājya upavītasthāne upavītaṁ saṁsthāpya
daṇḍhādibhiralaṁkṛtya mūrtipūjāṁ kṛtvā
trimadhuraṁ naivedya prasannapūjāṁ kṛtvā
tīrthaprokṣaṇāntam nīrājya agniṁ mṛdaṅge uddhāsya
layāṅgaṁ kuryāt
avasānīya — arghyaṁ datvā nīrājanamuddhāsya
gaṇeśaṁ visṛjya tadānīme mārdaṅgiko
vastraṁ datvā mṛdaṅgaṁ pravṛtya tāḍayet
and
[*atra ācāryaḥ svayameva prathamataḥ praṇavena,*
hom nama iti mantreṇa, namaḥ śivāya
śabdatanmātrātmane namaḥ ityanena mantreṇa
ca svayam vādayet iti pakṣāntaraṁ asti.]

8

Śuddha Maddaḷam

MADDAḶAM is a drum of great antiquity. The original Sanskrit name for this instrument is seen as *mardala* and the derivation of this word is given as *marda lāti mardala* (that which receives blows). The antiquity of the instrument can be known from the fact that it is mentioned even in the *Mahābhārata* (8.44.16):

> *mṛdaṅgānakaśaṅkhānām mardalānāṁ ca nisvanaiḥ* |
> *kharoṣṭraśvataraiścaiva mattāyāsyāmahe sukham* ||

Bharata's *Nāṭyaśāstra* gives an interesting story of the origin of drums. The sage Svāti went to fetch water from a lake. A sudden rain came and Svāti noticed that the falling of the rain drops on lotus leaves produced different tones of sound. Going back to the hermitage he devised the *mṛdaṅga*.

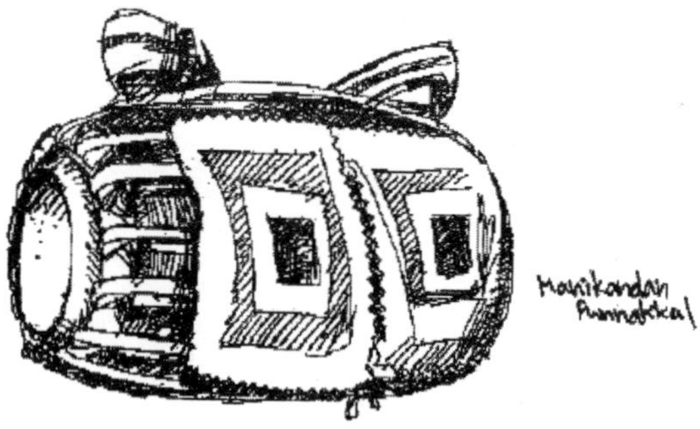

Maddaḷam

In Kerala, a mythological story is current, which says that while Lord Śiva was doing the *tāṇḍava* during the *pradoṣa* period, Nandikeśvara took a broken pillar and shaped a drum out of it which resulted in the *maddaḷam*. Due to the association of *maddaḷam* with the cosmic dance of Śiva it is called a *deva vādya* in contradistinction to *asura vādya*s which are not used in temple rituals though they may be used in temple festivals. This association of divinity, particularly of Śiva[1] is expressed in the *Saṅgīta Makaranda*:

> *dakṣiṇāgre sthito rudra umā vāme pratiṣṭhitā* ।
> *śivaśaktimayo nādo mardale parikīrtitaḥ* ।।

> Śiva is present on the right side and Umā on the left of the *maddaḷam* and the sound from the *maddaḷam* is divine.

In the *Nāṭyaśāstra* while *mṛdaṅga* and other instruments are mentioned, *mardala* is not mentioned specifically. It is however mentioned in the *Saṅgīta Ratnākara*. Several verses are devoted to its specifications, construction and the mnemonics for playing it,[2] *atha mardalaṁ lakṣayati, nirdoṣabījavṛkṣothaḥ*, etc., etc. the first portion of which may be summarized as follows: Wood of a good fruit tree has to be used for the barrel. Thickness is to be ½ finger, length 21 fingers, left face 14 fingers and right 13 fingers. The middle of the body should be thicker by a finger; circular thick hides are to be fixed on either side, forty holes to be made in the rim of the leather and fastened by hide strips interlocked in a zig-zag manner. Rings are to be fixed on either end and through these rings a silk or other attractive cloth-bend has to be passed and tied to the waist for playing.

1. See Appendix.
2. See Appendix.

Such an instrument is called a *mardala, mṛdaṅga* or *muraja.* Suitable minerals have to be mixed with rice-paste and applied to the left face in a thick layer like a *pūri* and the other face has to be lightly smeared; and it produces thunderous sounds. The mnemonics used are *dhi theim daim nam dam*, etc., etc.

The *Saṅgīta Dāmodara* gives almost the same but even a more lucid description in:[3] *mardalaḥ khādiraḥ śreṣṭho hīnaḥ syādanyadārujaḥ*, etc. which can be summarized as follows: *khādira* wood (*Acacia catechu*) is best for *mardala*; others are inferior but red sandalwood gives a superior sound. It should be one and a half hands long. The right end should be 13 or 12 fingers and the left less by half or one finger. The ends should be covered with hide. The middle of the barrel should be bigger than the ends. The hide used is to be taken of a 6 month old goat. When the body is made of mud it is called *mṛdaṅga*. A paste made of holy ash, minerals, rice, the fruit (or root ?) of a particular astringent plant should be applied thick and should be made to hold fast on the right end; it should merely be smeared on the left end. This is how the superior instrument *mardala* is made. When it is played with other instruments it enlivens them.

In the *Nāṭyaśāstra* it is mentioned that *mṛdaṅga* gets its name because it is made of *mṛd* (mud). From these it will be seen that the old Sanskrit texts do not make any material distinction between *mṛdaṅga* and *mardala*. It is possible that instruments of different sizes, though of the same construction, were known by different names and it is also likely that the distinction was brought about later.

---

3. See Appendix.

In Tamil the instrument is known as *maddaḷam* and seems to have been popular in Tamil Nadu even during the Saṅgam period. During the period known as the Golden Age of Carnatic Music we hear of one Thambiappan attached to Tiruvārūr temple, who was a disciple of Muthuswamy Dikshitar and who was an expert *śuddha maddaḷam* player. It is reported that *śuddha maddaḷam* is played at Tiruvārūr temple always whenever the chief deity Tyāgaraja is taken out in the festival and also at the daily services before this deity. Another instrument known as *pañchamukha vādya* was also in use in Tiruvārūr temple.

In Malayalam the instrument is known as *maddaḷam* though in some old manuscripts it is even referred to as *matthaḷam, matthaḷi* or *matthuli.*[4] While its use in Tamil Nadu is rare, it is widely used in Kerala during temple rituals and temple festivals. The shape of the *maddaḷam* in Kerala is similar to the *mṛdaṅga* though in the construction and playing there are a few significant differences. There are three types of *maddaḷam* in Kerala, *toppi maddaḷam, vīra maddaḷam* and *śuddha maddaḷam*. Essentially the difference is only in the size and naturally in the use to which they are put. All the three types of *maddaḷam* are tied round the waist for playing. The *Nāṭyaśāstra* mentions three types of instruments, *aṅkya, āliṅgya* and *ūrdhvaka*, i.e. the instruments played by (i) keeping them on the lap, (ii) keeping them in an embracing position, and (iii) keeping them in an upright position. According to this, *maddaḷam* will come under the *āliṅgya* type. In the case of *toppi maddaḷam,* some used to hang it over the shoulders (as the sacred thread is worn), keep it in an inclined position and play it.

---

4. Malayalam translation of *Amarakośa* in palm leaf manuscript.

Toppi Maddaḷam

In size and construction it is similar to the *mṛdaṅga*. It does not have the *mīṭṭu* leather as in the *mṛdaṅga* and the bulge in the barrel is in the middle. No rice paste is applied to the left end.

Toppi maddaḷam is normally used for rituals inside the temple. It is also used in art forms like Oṭṭan Tuḷḷal and Kuṛatti Āṭṭam. It is being replaced by the *mṛdaṅga*.

Vīra Maddaḷam

As its very name suggests, it is obviously intended for *vīra rasa* and is associated with royalty. For example, in every ritual and function connected with the *Mahārājā*s of Cochin, the *vīra maddaḷam* has to be played. It is truly a king-size instrument and one may aptly apply the Vedic sentence in describing it, *rūpamevasaitanmahimānam vyāchaṣṭe* (its very appearance will make clear its superiority). It was used during military marches and campaigns and during *Attachchamayam* procession of the *mahārājā* of Cochin — this procession being a commemoration of a victory of their dynasty. For the elephant procession of Trippayar Tevar (Śrī Rāma), for the famous Arattupuzha Pūram, *vīra maddaḷam* is used, the idea being that Śrī Rāma is received with royal honours. In the southern districts of Kerala this instrument was being used by a community known as *pāṇa*s, a scheduled caste people who are professional singers; one type of their song is called "Tukiluṇarttuka" (a sort of carol singing).[5]

5. Normally "Panas" use only the drum known as *uṭukku* (*ḍhakka*).

Śuddha Maddaḷam

Then we come to the standard *maddaḷam*. The normal size of an instrument is about 27 inches long and the diameter at the two ends is about 11 and 10 inches. A ridge protrudes outside round the middle of the barrel. Normally jackwood is used to make the barrel, but *konna* (*Cassia fistula*) and *veṅga* (*Pterocarpus marsupium*) are also used. The right face (the black coloured bigger face) is covered with ox-hide and the left face (white, smaller) is covered with water-buffalo hide. These faces are fixed tight with buffalo-hide circular caps which are then tightened with buffalo-hide straps as is done in the *mṛdaṅga*.

It is reported that formerly both faces were of ox-hide. In the construction of temples and even houses there are restrictions on the relation between the length and breadth of buildings and even rooms according to the Śāstras. Similar restrictions were observed in the constructions of musical instruments also. For example, the length of a drum and the diameter of its face should satisfy the *yoni*-relations.[6] Of course, when instruments are made by unlettered

---

6. In books of Temple Architecture, etc. the term *yoni* is explained as the balance obtained by adding the length and breadth and multiplying it by three and dividing by eight. Only if the *yoni* obtained is an odd number the dimensions are approved. Even number *yoni*s are taboo. See *Tantrasamuccaya:*

   iṣṭātānavitānamānanicaye trighnéṣṭabhirbhājite
   śeṣo yoniḥ . . .
   dhvajo dhūmaśca simhaśca śunako vṛṣabhastathā |
   kharaścaiva gajaścaiva vāyaso vāstuyonayaḥ | |

   ādiprabhṛticatvāra ekaikāntaritāḥ śubāḥ |
   dvitīyādyāstathaivānye catvārastvaśubhāḥ smṛtāḥ | |

artisans they usually follow the dimensions of an instrument known to be good.

The tightening of the straps and the tuning of the *maddaḷam* is an arduous task. The hides have first to be soaked in water for several hours and three persons, heavy hammers and pegs are required to bring them to proper tension. One *maddaḷam* requires almost all the hide from a water buffalo. A paste made from carbon obtained by burning arecanut palm fronds and *purāṇakiṭṭam* (iron slag) and cooked raw rice is applied in a thick circular layer on the right end and the juice of raw betel nut is rubbed on to make the paste adhere better. On the left face of the instrument nothing is applied. Formerly there used to be 16 holes on each end cap for tightening the straps as in the case of the *mṛdaṅga*. Now 17 or 18 holes are made.

Unlike the *mṛdaṅga* it is not possible to adjust the *śruti* in the middle of a performance. But once the *śruti* is set it does not alter easily. The *maddaḷam* is tied round the waist with a long piece of cloth passed through hide-rings fixed to the ends of the drum. The drum is kept in a horizontal position and played with both the hands. Fingering is much lesser than in the *mṛdaṅga*. Fingers, particularly the right hand ones, are covered with gummed cloth-rings and caps for protection and for louder sound.

In keeping with the size of the instrument and its use in open space, the force of the beats is much harder and justifies the Sanskrit name *mardala* fully. The average weight of the instrument is 37 lbs. and one can very well understand the strain that is involved for an artist in not only playing for hours together with the instrument tied to his waist but also walking with it in processions. A couple of decades ago, it was not uncommon for the same *maddaḷam* artist to play non-stop from 9 p.m. to 6 a.m. in Kathakali performances.

Apart from the difference in size and the origin of the hides used, one important difference between the *maddaḷam* and the *mṛdaṅga* is that the *mīṭṭu* leather is not found in the *maddaḷam*. Also the black pasted end in the *mṛdaṅga* is played with the right hand whereas in the *maddaḷam*, it is played with the left hand. Because of the bigger size and the greater quantity of the black paste applied, it gives a deeper and more resonant sound.

Maddaḷam is used during temple rituals, in temple festivals, elephant processions, in Kathakali, in Kṛṣṇāṭṭam play and in some folk arts in Kerala.

Methods of Teaching

One may wonder as to how a young boy — the training starts even before a boy is in his teens — would start learning on such a heavy and big instrument. This difficulty is easily solved by using a dummy instrument for the trainee. This is called a *śravaṇa palaka* (literally a plank for hearing). This consists of two small planks held in a vertical position and joined together in the middle by a length of reaper. The following mnemonics (*cholkeṭṭu*) are used:

First Lesson: *tha thi thom nam* — This is very similar to the first lessons of the *mṛdaṅga*

Second Lesson: *tha tha thi thi thom thom nam nam*

Third Lesson: *dhikkinna dhikkinna dhi dhi dhi kinna dhikkinna dhim* All these are practised in four tempos.

Dhimṛta Lesson: *dhi tha ka na dhi tha ka na kkinna dhim tha ki na dhee tha ki nna kinna*. This is for good practice of the left hand.

Lesson for practice of fingers: *tha kki nna ki ta tha ki tha tha kki nnna ki ta tha ki*

After the practice of such preliminary lessons the student is taught the playing of *keḷi*. There are two types of *keḷi*s. One is *sandhyā keḷi* performed in temples after the evening *dīpārādhana*. This is part of the festival rituals known as *viḷakku-āchāram*. In this one *maddaḷam*, one *cheṇṭa* and a pair of *ilattāḷam*s do *laya-vinyāsa* in *chempaṭa tāḷa*. This can last from 15 minutes to one hour or more, depending on the time available and the ability of the player. While set mnemonics are taught, there is also scope for improvisation. This type of *keḷi* is also played at sunset at the venue of a Kathakali, there being a slight difference in the beginning of the playing.

Another type of *keḷi* is performed during Kathakali before the play starts. One of the two *maddaḷam*s play *laya-vinyāsa*. *Tāḷa*- accompaniment is by *ilattāḷam* and *cheṅgila*. Only *chempaṭa tāḷa* is played (*ādi tāḷa*). *Tiśra*, *miśra* and *khaṇḍa naḍai*s are played under the name of *kūrū vāyikkal*. Towards the end before the playing of the finale, one *cheṇṭa* also joins them to keep time — just to give a forceful effect. Immediately after this *keḷi* the *maddaḷam* is again played (with an *ilattāḷam* accompaniment), the play being called *choriṭṭa kai*. The *tāḷa* is *ādi tāḷa*, but the treatment is different from the playing of the *keḷi* and the duration is only a few minutes

During temple festivals, especially at night when the deity is brought out for elephant-procession round the temple, performances on individual instruments are played. There will be *tāyampaka* on the *cheṇṭa*, then there will be *paṟṟu*[7] on the *maddaḷam*. *Paṟṟu* is only *laya-vinyāsa* on the *maddaḷam* and it is the same as the *keḷi* before the start of Kathakali. It is known under a different name since the occasion is different. A *paṟṟu* for name's sake may last only for 5 minutes in small temples. In big ones it may last for one or one and half hours. Normally three instruments take part, but in former days in temples like Tripunithura (family temple of the Cochin *mahārājās*) as many as 30 instruments used to play together. In such a large ensemble, unless the artists are properly trained, the chances of harmonious blending are poor. Three or five instruments are normal and produce good effect. In some places one *cheṇṭa* also joins the *maddaḷam* during the *paṟṟu*.

In playing the *paṟṟu* the various stages of the tempos are known as (1) *viḷamba kālam*, (2) *eṭanila*, (3) *eṭa kālam*, (4) *pathiñña-erikiṭa*, and (5) *muṟukiya nila*. Mnemonices for each stage is taught, which the student can elaborate by improvisation according to his ability. Different *naḍai*s are played during the *vilambakālam* and this is known as *kūṟu vāyikkal*. *Pañcheri kūṟu* is *tiśra*, *aṭanta kūṟu* is *miśra* and *chempa kūṟu* is *khaṇḍa*.

One of the most important uses of the *maddaḷam* is in the *pañchavādyam* ensemble of Kerala. There are two types of *pañchavādyas* — one for rituals like *Iṭakka Pradakṣiṇam* and another for festivals. In the *Kriyāṅga Pañchavādyam* the smaller *toppi maddaḷam* is used along with *iṭakka*, *śaṅkha*, *timila*, *cheṇṭa* (the booming right side alone is played), *kompu*,

7. The playing of *paṟṟu* on *maddaḷam* is the same as *tāyampaka* on the *cheṇṭa*. See article on *cheṇṭa*.

kuḻal and *ilattāḷam*. It is now performed as a ritual with little emphasis on the art.

For *sevāṅga pañchavādyam* used for temple processions, for reception of VIP's and so on, the instruments used are *śaṅkha, iṭakka, timila, maddaḷam, kompu* and *ilattāḷam*. Formerly the *kuḻal* was also being used but not so now. About fifty years ago (1922) the *maddaḷam* was not having the prominence it now has in *pañchavādyam*.[8] It used to be played only on one side in the vertical position, similar to the use of *timila*. It was Sri Venkitachala Iyer (alias Venkichan Swamy) of Tiruvilvamala[9] and his disciple Madhava Warrier who brought about a revolution by playing the *maddaḷam* in the horizontal position for *pañchavādyam* also, as was being done for playing *paṟṟu*, *keḷi*, etc. Venkichan Swamy also systematized the playing of *pañchavādyam* and his system is followed to this day. Our artist here, Sri Appukutty Poduval is a direct and the topmost disciple of Venkichan.

---

8. It is regretted that in some books written by some eminent authors, a mistake has crept in since *maddaḷam* is left out from *pañchavādyam* of Kerala and *cheṇṭa* is given in its place.

9. The Malayalam *śloka* (ascribed to Mahārāja Parīkṣit of Cochin) quoted below would go to show the eminence of Venkichan Swamy in *maddaḷam*:

   tiṅkaḷkkalādharanumāpati modamoṭe
   śaṅkiccitāte varamekukakāraṇattāl

   veṅkichchanennu pukal poṅṅiya vipranoṭi-
   nnaṅkattināyoruvanilliha maddaḷathil

   (Since Lord Śiva has blessed in full measure the famous brāhmin, Venkichan cannot be met with in combat by any one in *maddaḷam*).

A *pañchavādyam* performance lasts from one hour to four hours or more. It is played in the *tripuṭa tāḷa* but till the tempo is brought to a quick level, the *tāḷa* will appear as *ādi tāḷa* since only *chaturaśra naḍai* is played and the *tāḷa* is divided into units of 8 *mātrā*s. One *tāḷavaṭṭam* in the first *ativilamba* stage consists of 1792 *mātrā*s and it will take about 15 minutes to play one *tāḷavaṭṭam*. The second stage is 896 *mātrās*, the third 448 and the tempo is increased to 3½ *mātrā*s for the final *atidruta* stage. In playing the *pañchavādyam* in each stage, first all instruments will play together, then there will be competitive *vinyāsa* between *maddaḷam* and *timila* artists. Then all the instruments will play together and finish in a *kūṭṭikoṭṭal* (*muttāyippu*). The change of tempo from 1792 *mātrā*s to 3½ *mātrā*s is not in stages of having the *mātrā*s but only in slow degrees akin to the increase in tempo in the *bhajana*s of south India.[10]

The most important role of *maddaḷam* is in Kathakali and it can be classified under the following heads:

1. *Keḷi*: This is *laya-vinyāsa* on the *maddaḷam* and a *cheṇṭa* with *ilattāḷam* to keep time and is done at sunset at the venue of the Kathakali. It serves as an announcement that Kathakali is going to be performed at night.

2. *Araṅgu Keḷi*: Immediately after the lamp is lighted on the Kathakali stage a *śuddha maddaḷam* is brought and placed near the lamp. The artist then comes and takes the instrument after prayer, sounds both sides and then only fixes it on his waist. The *maddaḷam* artist has to perform throughout the Kathakali and the only rest he gets is when *śloka*s are recited. He then plays the *araṅgu keḷi* (*keḷi* on the stage) of *śuddha maddaḷam*.

---

10. See the article on *timila* for the *pañchavādyam*.

Tāḷa	*Mātrās*	*Equivalent in Carnatic Music*
Chempaṭa	8	*Chaturaśrajāti tripuṭa* (*ādi*)
Aṭanta	14	*Khaṇḍajāti aṭa*
Muṟi aṭanta	7	*Tiśrajāti tripuṭa* (also *Tiśra chāpu*)
Pañchāri	6	*Chaturaśrajāti rūpaka*
Chempa	10	*Miśrajāti jhampa*
Eka	1	*Eka*

3. Before the start of the actual Kathakali, there is an item called *meḷappadam*. The musician sings the *Aṣṭapadi "Mañjutara-Kuñjatala"* in the *jhampa tāḷa* to the accompaniment of *cheṇṭa* and a *maddaḷam*. Here the *cheṇṭa* and *maddaḷam* artists get an opportunity to exhibit their skill individually and in unison. At the end of the song the *cheṇṭa* and the *maddaḷam* (without the musician) take the stage and play *laya-vinyāsa* in *chempaṭa tāḷa*. This brings out the best in the artists.

4. The most significant role of *maddaḷam* is as an accompaniment to the music and dance of Kathakali. While the male characters take the stage (*tāṇḍava*) both the *cheṇṭa* and *maddaḷam* are played but when the female characters take the stage (*lāsya*), only *maddaḷam* is played. Kathakali music and dance are set to different *tāḷa*s and *naḍai*s and only in Kathakali does the artist get an opportunity to play the *tāḷa* other than *chempaṭa* and *tripuṭa*. The *tāḷa*s are the same as in classical Carnatic Music, though known under different names.

While the *pada* is being sung the *maddaḷam* has to play as an accompaniment for the music. After each *charaṇa* of the *pada* the actor does a dance (*kalāśam*) where the *maddaḷam* has to accompany the dance. After the *pada*s are sung and acted, sometimes the actors converse in sign language to bring out details left out in the *padas*. Sometimes a single character on the stage will have the soliloquy or may render a description of what he sees around, all in sign language. This is known as Ilakiyāṭṭam and Tantetāṭṭam. The *maddaḷam* artist has to give the proper background for all this. In Kathakali, rhythm is supreme, every action of the artist should be rhythmic and it falls on the *maddaḷam* (and *cheṇṭa*) to give the proper accompaniment.

Another interesting aspect of *maddaḷam* playing in Kathakali is the interpretation in sound of the action and gestures of the actor. For example, the actor shows a lotus flower opening out, a bee or a butterfly coming and enjoying the honey, the cuckoo cooing in the garden, lovers coming into the garden, the lover tuning the *mṛdaṅga* and his fiancee tuning a *vīṇā* and playing. All these are translated into sound by the competent *maddaḷam* artist. How effectively this could be done, has to be seen, to be believed.

Kṛṣṇāṭṭam

Also known as Kṛṣṇanāṭṭam, this is a dance drama normally performed only at the Guruvayur temple. It is the story of Kṛṣṇa's life and the text followed is *Kṛṣṇagīti* of Manaveda (a Zamorin of Calicut). Kṛṣṇāṭṭam is even older, though a bit primitive than Kathakali. In this, the main *tāḷa* accompaniment is the *maddaḷam*. One *maddaḷam* is *śuddha maddaḷam* and the other is a *toppi maddaḷam*, though bigger than the small *toppi maddaḷam* detailed before. The function of the *maddaḷam* is the same as in Kathakali, namely to accompany the songs and dance. In Kṛṣṇāṭṭam *cheṇṭa* is not used.

Folk Arts

Śuddha Maddaḷam is not normally used in folk arts but in some processions connected with folk arts, *pañchavādya* is played. In Pālghāṭ district in Kerala, there used to be staged "Mīnākṣi-kalyāṇa" done in a mixture of Kathakali and drama styles. *Śuddha maddaḷam* is reported to have been used in its staging.[11]

From the demonstration given by the artist it would be clear that *śuddha maddaḷam* deserves more popularity than it has at present, especially outside Kerala. It would be a suitable accompaniment for outdoor performances. It is gratifying to note that many dance troupes and cinema orchestras have already started using *śuddha maddaḷam.*

There are a few training institutions in Kerala for *śuddha maddaḷam.* The Kerala Kalamandalam is the foremost of these institutions where systematic training is imparted for a course of four years under the able personal instruction of the artist here, Sri Appukutty Poduval. As in the case of most other instruments, there are no books available on the subject. Encouragement of bodies like the Music Academy of Madras should induce an eminent artist-cum-teacher like Sri Poduval to put in his profound knowldge for the benefit of posterity.

Appendix

From Śārṅgadeva's *Saṅgīta Ratnākara — Ṣaṣṭho Vādyādhyāyaḥ*

atha mardalam lakṣayati —

---

11. See S.K. Nair, *Keralathile Nāṭōṭi Nāṭakaṅgaḷ* (Folk Plays of Kerala).

nirdoṣabījavṛkṣottaḥ piṇḍe ardhāṁgulasaṁmitaḥ ।
ekavimśyatyāṅgulaḥ syāddairghe vāme mukhe punaḥ ।।

caturdaśāṅgulāni syurdakṣiṇe tu trayodaśa ।
mānam yasya manāṅmadhyah pṛthurekāṅgulādhike ।।

vaktrābhyām carmaṇī vṛtte ghane ye prāntayotsayoḥ ।
catvāriṁśatpṛthagrantrāṇyaṅgulāntaravanti ca ।
vadhre tadrantravinyaste sīvanaprakriyāvati ।।

protodhvārdhaḥ sthitā dṛṣṭodarapṛṣṭhā ca vignikā ।
kriyate veṣṭyate madhye tribhirbandhairdṛḍhaṁ tathā ।।
kāryā gomūrtikābandhastatra vadhradvayena ca ।।

tathā yathā pinaddhāsye bhavetāṁ carmaṇi dṛḍhe ।
kuṇḍalyo prāntayorvāmakuṇḍalyām saṁniveśya ca ।।

kacchāṁ kṣiptvā dakṣiṇāsyām kṛṣṭvā dviguṇatāṁ nayet ।
sañcaladvitayām paṭṭamayimaṣṭaṅgulāyatām ।।

yadvā 'nyavastrajam śobhānugām nyasyetkaṭītaṭe ।
nigadanti mṛdaṅgaṁ taṁ mardalaṁ murajaṁ tathā ।।

proktaṁ mṛdaṅgaśabdena muninā puṣkaratrayam ।
atyantāvyavahāryartvānnihśaṅko na tanoti tat ।।

bhūtimiśrena bhaktena cikkaneṇātimardanāt ।
piṇḍikāṁ pūrikākārāṁ vāmavaktre niveśayet ।।

bohaṇākhyena tenāsyāṁ limpedalpena dakṣiṇam ।
evaṁ jaladharadvānagambhīro bhavati dhvaniḥ ।।

niḥśaṅkenātra ca prokto devatā nandikeśvaraḥ ।
raktachandanajo yadvā khādīro 'anyairayaṁ mataḥ ।।

triṁśadāṅguladairghaiśca piṇḍe tvaṅgulasaṁmitaḥ ।
etasya vāmaṁ vadanaṁ dvādaśāṅgulasaṁmitam ।।

dakṣiṇam tu mitaṁ sārddhairekādaśabhiraṅgulaiḥ ।
pāṭāśca taddhithoṭemhemnaṁdemityatra kīrtitāḥ ।।

From *Saṅgīta Dāmodara* as quoted in the *Śabdakalpadrum* —

mardalaḥ khādirah śreṣṭho hīnaḥ syādanyadārujaḥ ।
raktachandanajo ramyo ghabhīradhvaniruccakaiḥ ।।

sārdhahastapramāṇaṁ tu dairghyamasya vidhīyate ।
trayodaśāṅgulaṁ vāmamathavā dvādaśāṅgulam ।।

dakṣiṇaṁ ca bhavet hīnamekenārdhāṅgulena vā ।
kareṇānaddhavadano madhye cāiva pṛthurbhavet ।।

ṣaṇmāsīyo mṛto vastastaccarmakaraṇaṁ matam ।
mṛttikānirmitaścaiva mṛdaṅgaḥ parikīrtitaḥ ।।

pātayet kharalim vādyavādanārthaṁ ca mardale ।
vibhūtigaurikaṁ bhaktaṁ kāñjikena ca saṁyutaṁ ।।

yadvā cipiṭakaṁ deyaṁ jīvanīsatvamiśritam ।
sarvamekatra piṣṭam tallepaḥ kharalirucyate ।।

vāmāsye pūrikām kṛtvā lepaṁ dadyācca dakṣiṇe ।
evaṁ mardalakaḥ proktāḥ sarvavādyottamottamaḥ ।।

asya samyogamāsādya sarvaṁ vadyaṁ ca śobhate ।

mardalastrayodaśāṅgulavāmamukho dvādaśāṁgulada-kṣiṇamukhaḥ ।

murajastvaṣṭādaśāṅgulavāmamukhaḥ saptadaśāṅgula dakṣiṇamukhaḥ ।।

Demonstration of Śuddha Maddaḷam — The Artists

MADDAḶAM ARTIST

Sri Appukutty Poduval (born in 1099 ME (CE 1924)) belongs to Kandanchatu family and is the son of Sm. Kunjammalu Puduvalasyar and Sri T.S. Ramachandra Iyer. He belongs to Tiruvilvamala village which has produced many illustrious *laya vidvān*s (including Sri T.S. Mani Iyer). Sri

Poduval started learning *maddaḷam* at the age of 10 under the illustrious *maddaḷam* exponent Sri Venkichan Swamy (who was the uncle of Ghatam Vilvādri Iyer). He is now (1972) the chief Maddaḷam Instructor at the Kerala Kalamandalam and is considered the foremost artist for playing *maddaḷam* for Kathakali.

He has toured all over the world including England, France, Italy, Germany, Holland, Belgium, Switzerland, USA., Canada, Japan, Hong Kong, China, Australia, Indonesia, Malaya, Iran and Lebanon.

THE KATHAKALI ARTIST

Sri P.M. Sankaran Nambudiri joined the Kalamandalam after passing his pre-university exam. He had 8 years' training there for Kathakali acting and he had 2 years' training in Ceylon in Kandyan dance. He is now on the staff of the Kerala Kalamandalam. He has toured all over Europe, America, China, Japan, Indonesia, Iran, etc. with the Kathakali troupe of Kalamandalam and he has participated in many lecture-demonstrations.

THE TIMILA AND TĀḶAM ARTIST

Sri Annamanada Parameswara Marar is already known to the Music Academy as he had demonstrated the *timila* last year. He is the chief instructor in *timila* at the Kerala Kalamandalam and is the foremost authority on *pañchavādyam* in Kerala. He is currently engaged in giving final shape to his book on *pañchavādyam*.

APPENDIX - A

Folk Musical Instruments of Kerala

KERALA is rich in the number and variety of musical instruments and the richness of its legacy is not below that of any other region in India. Many instruments in use today were known to have been in use thousands of years ago as they are found mentioned in the earliest books. The very nature of music makes it a conservative and tradition-bound art. Any change that takes place is gradual and it is no wonder that many of the musical instruments now extant were known to have existed centuries ago.

Probably the earliest record of musical instruments in Kerala is that given in the celebrated Tamil classic *Śilappadikāram* believed to be written about two thousand years ago in Kerala. The following drums now in use are mentioned in *Śilappadikāram* — *iṭakka, maddaḷam, uṭukku, timila, mil̲āvu, par̲a,* and *tuṭi.*[1]

Many references are found in Malayalam literature about musical instruments. Though they may deal with the higher strata of society, they are essentially folk type in nature. One of the oldest works in Malayālam, *Uṇṇunīli Sandeśam,* believed to be written in the fourteenth century

1. Article on "Drums through the Ages" by S. Krishnaswamy of A.I.R., *Journal of the Music Academy*, Madras, 1967, gives the names of 29 drums mentioned in Śilappadikāram.

mentions the following instruments: *śauṇḍi, veṇu, stani, śabarika, paṅkitam, rāvaṇan kai, sāraṅgam, nantuṇi, niṟameḻuntaṇṇi, pinākam, vīṇā.*[2] Of these though only *veṇu, nanṭuṇi* and *vīṇā* are known in Kerala now, the important point is that the work mentions instruments which are still found in other parts of India. For example, *rāvaṇan kai* is found in Rajasthan as *rāvaṇ hatha, sāraṅgam* is found not only in north India as *sāraṅgī* but even in the temples of Tinnevelly, Courtallam and Tenkasi. Some areas like Shenkottah, Courtallam, etc. until recently, were part of Travancore state.

In a manuscript of *Amarakośa* with a Malayalam commentary, the following Malayalam equivalents of Sanskrit names of instruments are given: *ḍamarū* (*kaṭum tuṭi*), *ḍiṇḍimam* (*paṟa* and/or *cheṇṭa*), *jharjara* (*vallari paṟa*), *paṇava* (*nada miḻāvu*).[3]

Tuñcatt Eluttacchan in his *Mahābhāratam Kiḷippāṭṭu* mentions several instruments used in the Mahābhārata War. These may be taken as the equivalents of the ones mentioned in the original (Sanskrit) *Mahābhārata*: *takil, muraśu, paṟa, paṭaham, tuṭi, saṅkha, tammiṭṭam, nakra, maddaḷam, vīṇā, kuḻal, kāhaḷam, śṛṅgam, iṭakka,* and *uṭukku*. Most of these are still in use in Kerala.[4]

---

2. *Uṇṇunīli Sandeśam,* Pūrva Bhāgam, verse 19:

   śauṇḍī, veṇu, stani, śabarikā, paṅkitam, rāvaṇankai
   śāraṅgam, nanṭuṇi niṟameluntaṇṇi, vīṇā, pinākam
   maṟṟum vādyolkkaram anutarikinṟa gītāmṛtam te

3. *Pañchika* commentary for *Amarakośa* in a palm-leaf manuscript with Āḻuvāñcery Tambrākkaḷ. Reference obtained through the help of Pandit K.P. Narayana Pisharoti.

4. *Mahābhāratam Kiḷippāṭṭu,* Bhīṣma Parvam:

   takil muraśu paṟa paṭaha tuṭikaḷoṭu śaṅkhavum →

In the Malayalam work, *Chandrotsavam* (believed to be 400 to 500 years old) there is a reference to *ṭappu* (a kind of drum). *Ṭappu* is also mentioned in some of the children's songs.[5]

Kuñchan Nambiar, who invented the folk art form known as Ōṭṭan Tuḷḷal refers to a number of instruments in his Tuḷḷal works.[6] While many of them are still in use, some

---

→ *tammiṭṭavum nakramaddaḷam vīṇāyum*
madhuratara mṛdularasa ninadakuḻal kāhaḷam
maṟṟu śṛṅgangaḷiṭaykkayuṭukkukaḷ

5. *Chandrotsavam*, 4th Sarga, verses, 29 and 30.

tadanu puṭa puḻaṅṅī tappu pilpāṭukūṭe, etc., etc.
okkaddikkuñjarāṇām cevi poṭi peṭumāralbhutam tappu koṭṭi, etc., etc.

Both these verses depict *tappu* as producing extremely big sound. In contrast a song used to induce childern to eat their food would indicate that *tappu* is a milder drum:

tappo tappo tappāni
tappo tappo tappāni
tappu kilinkilum tāḷam kilinkilum
tappāri koṭṭi valaññu varunpoḷ
tappukuṭukkelentuṇṭu
nārāṇan vecca kaṟiyuṇṭu
naññeli kācciya mōruṇṭu
uṇṇikkuṇṇān cōruṇṭu
accan vanne uṇṇāvu
māvum māvum māvum

In fact, there are two instruments known as *tappu* to suit the above two descriptions.

6. Kuñchan Nambiar's Tuḷḷal compositions:

(a) ***Bāṇayuddham***

→

are quite unfamiliar now in Kerala: *ambiḷivaḷa, ghaṭṭu vādyam, jhallari, jharjharam, ḍiṇḍimam, maḍḍu, mukha-vīṇā,* and *muraśu*. It is also significant that Kuñchan Nambiar has mentioned Tamberu. Tamberu is now the name used

---

→ *tittiyiṭakkayuṭukkum timilakaḷ*
ottum maddaḷametravidhattil
kāḷam cēṅgila cheṇṭakaḷ timilakaḷ
nīḷam kuṛayum kompum kuḻalum
ambiḷivaḷayam tamberenniva
meḷam koṇṭu jagattu muḻakki.

Ambiḷivaḷa is said to be still found in Trivandrum area and seems to be the Chandrapirai (a crescent shaped ring in which parchment is fixed) beaten with two sticks. Ambiḷivaḷayam refers to Candravaḷayam vide *Rāmakatha Pāṭṭu*, Dr. P.K. Narayana Pillai, vol. 1 (N.B.S., Kottayam)

(b) ***Syamantakam:***

tappumaddaḷamitakkayuṭukkukaḷ
tittivīṇā mukhavīṇa muraśum
cheṅgila timila nalla mṛdaṅgam
cheṇṭa kaṭuntuṭi kaṇṭham jālam
ḍiṇḍimamamkyamiṭakkayuṭukkukaḷ
maḍḍu jallarikal jarjara vādyam
ittaram vividha vādya samūham
pattulakṣamivayokke muḻakki

(c) ***Dhruvacaritam:***

maddaḷakkāruṭe koṭṭum kalāśavum
kūttiniṇaṅṅunna titti prayōgavum

kāḷam kaṭuntuṭi cheṅgilayum nalla
meḷam takilum muraśum kalāvidya

(d) ***Satyā Svayamvaram:***

koṭṭumkuḻal viḷikkoṭṭum kuṛavumilla
taṭṭummukaḷil cila koṭṭutappinṟe ghōṣam

rather loosely, for western side-drum and also for the Tambourine used by the Muslims of Malabar.

Other such references should be the subject of research as they would give some guidelines for the study of musical instruments. Unfortunately, the advent of western civilization has reduced the interest of the public, in general, in our old musical instruments so that even some of the sophisticated and near-classical instruments find few eminent artists playing them. The advent of higher education in general, the mania for white-collar jobs, the financial debacle of the temples consequent to the new land legislation have all contributed to the paucity of learners of these instruments. The time is already overdue for the establishment of an institution for the teaching, preservation and research in musical instruments.

Ancient Hindu musicologists have classified musical instruments into four broad divisions and this categorization has been accepted by western musicologists.[7] The divisions of *vādyas* (or instruments) are:

→ **(e)** ***Kṛṣṇa Līlā:***

koṭṭu tappum kuḻalkkārum tamburu
ghaṭṭivādyam pala villum vaṭikaḷum

kiñkiṇijālam kiluññunna śañkiccu

Ghaṭṭi vādyam may be the same as *gaṭṭu* (or *goṭṭu*) *vādyam* of Tamil Nadu a *tambūra* like instrument. The strings are beaten with 2 small sticks and used as an instrument for rhythm.

7. *Nāṭyaśāstra,* Chapter 28 on musical instruments:

tatam caivāvanaddhaṁ ca
ghanaṁ suṣirameva ca
caturvidhaṁ tu vijñeya

Ghanaṁ	:	Solid or Idiophonic or Autophonic
Avanaddhaṁ	:	Membrophonic or Skin
Suṣiraṁ	:	Aerophonic or Wind
Tataṁ	:	Chordophonic or String.

Ghanaṁ or Idiophonic Instruments

These are solid instruments which emit a sonorous note when struck.

KŌL

A pair of small polished tapering sticks of hard wood about a foot in length struck against each other. Used by children for Kolāṭṭam dances, Harijans in their processions, in Muslim Kol Kaḷi, Ivar Kaḷi, Kaṇṇiyār Kaḷi, Pūrakkaḷi, etc. In some varieties, jingle bells are found attached.

CHIPḶA KAṬṬA

Wooden clappers about six inches long used during devotional singing, *kathā prasaṅga*, etc. Jingle bells are attached to some and to others brass discs are attached to give a tinkling sound.

→ *mātodyaṁ lakṣaṇānvitam*

tataṁ tantrīkṛtaṁ jñeyam
avanaddhaṁ tu pauṣkaram
ghanaṁ tāḷastu vijñeyam
suṣiro vaṁṣa ucyate.

Manmohan Ghosh has translated it as: Regular musical instruments are of four kinds such as stringed (*tataṁ*), covered (*avanaddhaṁ*), solid (*ghanaṁ*) and hollow (*suṣiraṁ*).

(Among these) the stringed ones are those with string, the covered means the drums, the solid the Cymbals and the hollow the Flutes.

Another variety in the shape of a spade with a handle made of hard wood about 4 or 5 inches wide and ¼ inch thick is used by mendicants and beggars to accompany their singing. This is the same as the Tikkiri Kaṭṭai of Tamil Nadu but does not seem to be known by any specific name. An empty match box with a match-stick fixed to the side with a rubber string is often seen used by beggars. It all depends on the ingenuity of the people.

TĀḶAM

(a) The small variety known as the *kuḻi tāḷam* is a pair of bell metal discs about 2 or 3 inches in diameter depressed almost hemi-spherically, held by loops passing through a hole in the middle of the disc, one disc is struck against the other. Used for folk dances, etc.

(b) Slightly bigger but flatter discs with a depression in the centre through which a hole is drilled to pass a string, diameter about 3 inches, called also *kinnāram* and *jhālara*. Usually used for *bhajana*s, etc.

(c) Big ones made of bell metal, rough cast and forged to a shape about 6 inches diameter. Used for *cheṇṭa meḷam, pañchavādyam,* etc. The particular alloy used makes it possible to forge it and gives a clear ringing sweet sound.

CEṄGILA

A circular disc of rough cast and forged bell metal thick in the middle, struck with a wooden mallet, used for all temple rituals, for Kathakali, Kṛṣṇāṭṭam, etc. usual size 6 inches to 9 inches diameter.

CHILAMPU

(a) These are hollow anklets filled with metal pellets. Worn by temple oracles (*veḷichchappāṭu*) for their ritual dances (*velichchappāṭu tuḷḷal*).

(b) A variety which is held in the hand and shaken. It is smaller in size than the previous one and is known as *kaichilampu*. This is also used by temple oracles.

KIṄKIṆĪ

Jingle bells made of bell metal or bronze or brass with metal or stone pellets inside. A number of them strung on a tape are tied round the legs for dancing.

ARAMAṆI

Bigger jingle bells are tied round the waist by temple oracles during their ritual dance.

KIṆṆAM

This is a thin metal bowl (rough cast and forged) known as *ōlakkiṇṇam* about 6 inches diameter and is beaten with the blunt edge of a pen-knife. It is used as rhythmic accompaniment for folk singing (Brāhmaṇi Pāṭṭu). Sometimes thicker bronze bowls are also used.

MAṆI

This is a regular hand bell made of bell metal. Apart from use in temple rituals certain mendicants use it as rhythmic accompaniment. Size varies widely.

VILLU

Also known as *ōṇavillu* since playing it is a pastime during the *ōṇam* festival. This is a bow about 3 ft long made of bamboo or palmwood. A thin stick of the same material with knobs at either end is fixed into slots at the two ends of the bow. This piece is in place of the string in a bow. The tension of this can be varied by pressing with the hands while it is held between the shoulder and arm and this enables production of tonal variations when striking it with a stick. This has been raised to a virtuoso instrument playing complicated rhythms. It is used specially during the *Ōṇam* festival, for Kummāṭṭi Kaḷi, etc. (see also under Chordophones).

THE WATER-DRAWING WHEEL (VEḶḶAM KORUNNA CAKAṬA OR TUṬI)

A drum-shaped contraption made by fixing wooden slats to two equal sized circular wooden discs. This is used as a pulley for drawing water from wells. A couple of wooden balls put inside the drum strikes against the slats when it turns while drawing water. This gives a xylophonic effect and lightens the burden of drawing water. Though not strictly a musical instrument, it is significant in considering the development of musical instruments in Kerala.

KOKKARA

This is a serrated piece of iron over which another piece of iron is rubbed creating a grating noise. This is used by hill tribes or tribal dances for keeping time.

PONTI (ALSO KNOWN AS KOLMAṆI IN SOME AREAS)

This is a wooden rod about 18 inches long with 3 or 6 small *chilampu* type circular jingles fitted on top. When the rod is shaken up and down the jingles resound. It is used as rhythmic accompaniment by artisans in what is known as Ivar Kaḷi when *Mahābhārata* stories are recited and danced, round a lamp. This is similar to the jingle-cum-lance used by postal runners in olden days.

Suṣira Vādyas or Aerophonic Instruments

The number of wind instruments in Kerala is comparatively small.

ŚAṄKHA

This is the conch-shell. It is blown for ritualistic purposes in temples and during the playing of *pañchavādyam,* during the entrance scenes of divinity or royalty in Kathakali, etc. It is considered a sacred instrument.

KOMPU

This is a conical cast bronze tube in three parts fitted together to form a semi-circle. Two or three different notes are produced by altering the strength of blowing and this is used as an instrument for rhythm during *cheṇṭa meḷam, pañchavādyam,* etc. During temple festivals this is also played solo for a short time. Unlike other parts of India where similar instruments are used merely for giving a loud tone this instrument is used to play complicated rhythms in Kerala.

OṬAKKUḺAL

This is a flute made of a variety of bamboo or reed called *oṭa.* Two varieties are in use: end blown or side blown. It is mostly used as a toy normally sold at festivals. Some cowherds and shepherds can be seen playing it during their work. Length of one foot to 3 ft are found sometimes.

KUḺAL

It is also called *kuṟum kuḻal* (literally short pipe). It is a dimunitive type of *nāgasvaram* about 9 inches to 12 inches. It is smaller than the north Indian *śehnāī*. A bell metal bell shaped piece is attached at the bottom of the conical wooden pipe. It has a reed mouth-piece. It is mainly used as an instrument for rhythm during *cheṇṭa meḷam*. It is also used as an instrument for melodic music during festivals for solo playing called *kul̲al par̲r̲u* and during the performance of Kūṭiyāṭṭam.

A similar *kul̲al* used by the Par̲aya community is even smaller and has only 4 or 5 holes and the reed is made of palm-leaf. Only 3 or 4 notes are produced and this instrument is used during Kāḷī worship by this community and during harvest festivals like buffalo race, etc.

A similar instrument used by the Īl̲ava community especially in Pālghāṭ district is called *īl̲ava vādyam*. It is more refined than the *par̲ayan kul̲al* but not as refined as the *kur̲um kul̲al*. This is also used during festivals of Bhadrakāḷī temples. It was amusing to find one Par̲ayan using a textile bobbin as the barrel for his *kulāl*, quite ingenious but showing a lack of consideration for tradition.

TUTTI

This is a bag-pipe mainly used as a drone. It has practically disappeared from Kerala.

Tata Vādyas or Chordophonic Instruments

The number of stringed instruments in Kerala is also small. The most important in this class is the *puḷḷuvan vīṇā*.

PUḶḶUVAN VĪṆĀ

This is a small fiddle like instrument. It has a shallow circular wooden resonator with its top covered with the skin of the monitor lizard. It is about 2 ft in length, the diameter of the resonator is about 9 inches and the bow is about 2 ft. A single string made from the fibre of *amṛta* (a medicinal creeper) is fixed and tightened by a wooden peg. The bow also uses the same fibre, and 2 small round hollow jingles (*chilampu*) are attached to the end of the bow, shaking this helps to keep the rhythm. It is used by the Puḷḷuvan community in rendering songs in praise of the divine *nāgas* (snakes) and in the elaborate ritual known as *pāmpu tuḷḷal* performed to propitiate the divine snakes. As it has one string only some 3 or 4 notes are produced, the range of the melody of Puḷḷuvans is also comparatively small.

PUḶḶUVAN KUṬAM

This is an earthen pot with a circular opening at the bottom. The bottom is covered by parchment extending to the middle of the pot and is laced and tightened to a circular leather thong bellow at the opening of the mouth of the pot. Through the hole in the pot, and in the parchment a leather thong is passed and held tight by fixing it to a stick and held tight by pressing with the thighs of the player. The string is vibrated by a piece of wood and it produces a *brum brum* sound. Women Puḷḷuvans (Puḷḷuvatti) when playing this use a smaller sized pot about 14 or 15 litres capacity whereas when men use the instrument the pot will be about 3 or 4 times bigger. Stronger quality pots (than ordinary water pots of villages) have to be used. This is used by the Puḷḷuvan community as an instrument for rhythm for their songs of snake worship. (This instrument may also be classified under the *avanaddha vādyas* or covered instruments — Membrophones).

NANTUṆI

This is described by some as a guitar of Kerala. It has a rectangular hollow wooden body with a tail-like projection. Two fibre strings are stretched over the body supported on bridges tied to an iron hoop at the one end and tightened by a peg at the other. It is used as a *śruti*-cum-*tāḷa* (drone-cum-rhythm) instrument. The Maṇṇān and Kuṟup communities use it mainly for Bhagavatī worship. The Maṇṇān community sing songs of the Kaṇṇaki legend whereas the upper class Kuṟup community use it for Devī worship in some temples, known as Kaḷam Eḻuttu Pāṭṭu, etc. Total length of the instrument would be about 4½ ft, width 6 inches, resonator length about 14 inches. A few frets are provided at about the middle of the instrument. The player presses only one string when playing with a horn plectrum. The first full string acts as the drone and two or three notes are produced by pressing the second string on the frets. There is no attempt to play any tune on the instrument.

VILLU

One type of *villu* has been dealt with under *ghanaṁ vādyas*. There is another *villu* or bow which is about 5 or 7 ft long. A number of jingle bells are attached to the bow which may be resting on an earthen pot which acts as a resonator. The string is struck with a wooden rod held in each hand to accompany song and story-telling known as Villaṭiccān Pāṭṭu or Vilpāṭṭu particularly in the south Kerala region. A party of 4 or more artists participate in this.

Avanaddha Vādyas or Membrophonic Instruments

UṬUKKU

This has an hour glass shaped body. On both ends thin skins are fixed to round hoops and braced with strings. By pressing on the strings tension can be varied and this produces good tonal variations. It is played by beating on one side with the fingers, the other hand holds the instrument and press the tension strings. This is used for Ayyappan Pāṭṭu (by all communities), for Māriamman Pāṭṭu (mainly by Tamil speaking lower class communities) and for Tukiluṇarttu Pāṭṭu by the Maṇṇān community.

TUṬI

It is a bigger type of *uṭukku*. It is played by beating one side by a thin stick and the other hand manipulating the tension strings. It is usually used by low caste communities during Bhagavatī worship. It is slung from the shoulder by a piece of cloth.

IṬAKKA

In appearance, *iṭakka* is similar to *tuṭi*. This is considered a sacred instrument and is invariably used in all temple rituals. The barrel (about 9 inches) is not very narrow (as in the case of *uṭukku* and *tuṭi*).

Red sandalwood is considered best for the barrel. Two thin palmyrah fibres are fixed across the face of the barrel and when the skin covering this is beaten with a thin stick, it gives a vibratory effect. The instrument is decorated with a number of wooden balls of different colours hanging from the strings and 4 small round sticks are used to keep the bracing strings tight. The tonal variation is up to even two octaves and this enables some few experts to play music on it.

TIMILA

This has an elongated hour-glass barrel about 2 ft. It is suspended vertically from the shoulders at waist level. It is played on one side by two palms. This is primarily used for temple rituals. It has been developed into a sophisticated *tāḷa vādya* and is the chief instrument of *pañchavādyam.*

KAÑJIRA (OR GAÑJIRA)

This has a round wooden frame. Monitor lizard skin is fixed on one side and the other is open. It is used for *bhajana* singing and for music concerts. It seems to be popular only comparatively recently.

TAPPU

It is the same as *gañjira* but the size may be a bit bigger and goat skin may be fixed in place of lizard skin. The frame is held in one hand and played with the other. Muslims are often seen using it for some of their folk singing like Arbana Muṭṭu, by mendicants, etc.

A bigger instrument with much wider frame and thicker skin is found with the same name. This is beaten with a stick and emits a fairly big sound. In some cases, the barrel is made of metal (usually discarded paint or varnish drums). In Trichur district this is known as *cheṭṭi vādyam,* the Koṅkaṇī-speaking Kudumi Cheṭṭis (or Mūppans) call it Maggoda. It is used for folk festivals like Kāvaṭi Āṭṭam, Puli Kaḷi (Oṇam Tiger) and so on.

This is also called *muṟi cheṇṭa* in some localities.

MIḺĀVU

This is a big copper, brass or earthen pot with a narrow open neck covered with parchment.

The skin is first soaked and then tied with strings round the neck. On drying, it gets tight. It is played by beating with both hands. This instrument is used by the Nambiar community for Cākyār Kūṭṭu and Kūṭiyāṭṭam (the Sanskrit stage of Kerala).

KIṬU PIṬI (ALSO CALLED IṬUPIṬI)

This is a pair of bowl shaped wooden bodied drums. The leather is laced to the body and is played with two sticks. This is used as a second drum for *nāgasvaram* play in some temples and as a leading (or announcing) drum in some temple processions. This is similar in appearance to Kirikaṭṭai or Kundalam in Tamil Nadu.

DAMMANAM

This is similar in shape and construction to the Kiṭu Piṭi described above but is about 3 times bigger in size. The skin used is thicker and the stick for playing is also bigger. This is used in some temples (Vadakkunathan temple, Trichur) along with *nāgasvaram* during *pūjā* time.

NAGĀṚĀ

This is also similar in shape to the above two but very much bigger in size. It is carried in a cart to lead some processions especially church processions in Kerala. It used to be played at gates of royal palaces (Cochin royal palace at Tripunithura) at dawn and sunset as a sign of royalty.

PĀṆI MARAM

Pāṇi maram has a cylindrical barrel both ends being covered with leather and braced with leather straps.

This is primarily used for temple rituals known as Pāṇi Koṭṭal. An instrument of the same name and similar in all respects except that one face is well applied with black paste is used by the Paṟaya community for some of the dances connected with Devī worship. It is also called by them, *mattaḷam* and it produces tones similar to *maddaḷam*.

CHEṆṬA

This is the most versatile and pouplar instrument of Kerala so much so any drum is referred to generally as a (type of) *cheṇṭa*. It has a cylindrical wooden barrel with leather covering on both sides; leather is fixed to hoops and braced with thick cotton strings; and the strings are tightened by loops of smaller strings. One end is covered by a single piece of leather while the other is a single piece to which is pasted a number of concentric circular pieces of leather in diminishing diameter on the inside so that it is not visible outside. This is called the right end and it gives a booming sound. One stick and one hand is used or two sticks. The normal playing end is the left end but the right end is used for keeping time or for playing to mark some auspicious occasions as taking out of the deity or during the appearance of gods on the Kathakali stage, etc. It is used for all temple festivals and processions, for Kathakali and many folk forms. Even Christians use it for their processions, etc. *Cheṇṭa* is not part of the famous *pañchavādyam* of Kerala as wrongly given in some books (though written by eminent personalities).

Achchan cheṇṭa is a bit bigger *cheṇṭa* used in the southern parts of Kerala and gives a bigger sound. When the booming side of *cheṇṭa* is played it is sometimes referred to as *vīkkan cheṇṭa*. A bigger size *cheṇṭa* used in Annapūrṇeśvari temple (Cherukunnu, Cannanore district) is referred to as *paṭaha vādyam* there.

PAṞA

A smaller sized instrument similar to *cheṇṭa* is known as the *paṟa*. *Paṟa* is also the name of a measure (about 13 litres) and the size of the cylinder in *paṟa* would be about the size of a *paṟa*. It is used in Devī worship known as Pāna and also by lower castes in their rituals. Different sizes and ones used by different communities are known with appropriate prefixes as *cirupaṟa, velan paṟa*, etc.

TAVIL

It would appear that this instrument is a later introduction to Kerala from Tamil Nadu. This is used as drum accompaniment of *nāgasvaram*. It is used exactly as is done in Tamil Nadu.

VĪRANAM

This is a two faced drum which looks like a cross between a *cheṇṭa* and a *tavil*. It is regularly used in a few temples (Tiruvilvamala temple near Lakkiti railway station).

ĪLAṞA

This is a drum about 1 ft long and 9 inches diameter at the head. The body is Jackwood usually and it is slightly thinner in the middle than at the ends. Cow calf hide is fixed to bamboo rings and braced with leather straps. A strap is tied at the middle of the depressed belly which makes it more tight. One side is played with a small stick, the other side is boomed by rubbing with small bent twig. A gum applied on the skin helps to increase the booming sound. This is an instrument used by the Maṇṇān community in Devī worship (Kaḷam E̠luttu Pāṭṭu).

Another instrument of the same name but about half as bigger is used by the Pa̠raya community. They use strings for bracing instead of leather. The body may be bit bulging in the middle instead of being depressed as in the previous one and the leather is not fixed on rings but only laced to the body. This is also played by striking one end and rubbing the other. An instrument similar to *pa̠ra* used for Tolpāva Kūttu (leather puppets in Pālghāṭ district) is called *iṭava̠ra*.

MADDAḶAM

Maddaḷam is a two faced drum similar to the famous *mṛdaṅga* of south India. It has no *mīṭṭu* skin covering on the black pasted end like the *mṛdaṅga*. The body bulges in the middle and tapers to both ends quickly. Three varieties are seen:

(a) Toppi Maddaḷam

This is the smallest size of an average *mṛdanga*. It is used for Ōṭṭan Tuḷḷal, some temple rituals like *Iṭakka Pradakṣiṇam*, etc. Since it is very similar to *mṛdaṅga* it is being replaced by it and one rarely comes across this. In Kṛṣṇāṭṭam of Guruvayur an instrument of the same name and construction but a bit bigger is used. One side of this is constantly moistened to give a muffling effect.

(b) Śuddha Maddaḷam

This is the standard sized *mṛdaṅga*. It is used for *pañchavādyam*, Kathakali, Kṛṣṇāṭṭam, etc. It is a virtuoso instrument of classical level.

(c) Vīra Maddaḷam

It is even bigger in size but now rarely used. It was used during the marching of armies and for royal processions and rituals connected with royalty.

In considering the above, some instruments found in Kerala but normally used by people belonging to neighbouring areas are left out. These include Kuṭukuṭuppai, a tiny drum used by wandering fortune-tellers, U̱rumai (similar to *īlaṟa*) used by demonstrators of trained bulls *(appan kāḷai)*, *pampai* (a double drum used for Māriamman festivals), and *makuṭi* (Snake charmer's pipe). Instruments found in Kasargoḍ area have also not been surveyed.

Instruments like *vīṇā, mṛdaṅga, nāgasvaram,* etc. are left out because they are classical instruments. So also instruments of western origin like the violin, clarionet and the harmonium.

One would note that the number of instruments for melodic music in Kerala is small but the number for rhythm or *tāḷam* is large. The development of melodic music in Kerala is poorer than in neighbouring regions. Except for Kṛṣṇāṭṭam (Kṛṣṇagīti) and the Kathakali compositions (Āṭṭakathās) melodic music compositions are few. The instruments for melodic music in Kerala like the *kuṟum kuḻal* and the *puḷḷuvan vīṇā* are not sufficiently developed to raise them to classical level. As pointed out earlier the wooden water drawing pulley is familiar to the Keralites but they have not chosen to develop a Kastatarang.

The position of instruments for rhythm is quite the opposite. Not only are there a large number but many of them have reached classical level and what is more, even instruments for melodic music like the *kurum kulal* is adopted by the Keralite for rhythm accompaniment. It is generally conceded that in north Indian classical music, the emphasis is more on the melody than on the rhythm. In south Indian music, the emphasis on rhythm is more and when it comes to Kerala, rhythm completely overshadows melody.

What has been attempted here is only a survey and the list cannot be exhaustive. Regional variations in name, in construction, etc. would be found. The same instrument may be known by different names in different localities, and an instrument known by the same name in different localities may be different. There is also a tendency to deviate from traditional methods of making the instruments and hybridization may result.

Similar or same instruments are found in neighbouring states, some under different names. As such, there is an urgent need of not only doing detailed survey and research in the State but also co-ordinating the work with those in neighbouring states.

Acknowledgements

The author acknowledges with thanks the literature references obtained from Pandit K.P. Narayana Pisharoti, U.G.C. Professor, Kerala Varma College, Trichur; Sri V.S. Sharma, Lecturer in Malayalam, University Centre, Trivandrum; and Sri Chummar Choondal., Lecturer, St. Thomas College., Trichur.

APPENDIX - B

A Brief History of the Tāḷa Vādyas of Kerala

In the development of Musical Instruments in Kerala the *tāḷa vādyas* have far outstripped other instruments. While there does not seem to be any musical instrument for melodic music indigenous to Kerala (barring perhaps the Puḷḷuvan's fiddle-like instrument) the number and types of *tāḷa* instruments are so many and varied. All these *tāḷa vādyas* are connected with the temples in one form or other and even the folk instruments have a folk-ritual background. The method of playing these instruments is also peculiar to Kerala.

Bhadra Kāḷī (or Durgā) temples can be seen in almost every village of Kerala and these Kāḷī temples are said to be older than temples of other gods of the Hindu Pantheon. The worship of the divine mother in her terrible form might have been partly responsible for the predominance of the *tāḷa vādyas*. Another factor is the tāntric nature of the worship in the temples as evidenced by the two *śloka*s from *Tantrasamuccaya* of Chennas Nambudiri.

Śloka 230

śaṅkhapreṅkhaccaṭulapaṭahottāḷatāḷorubherī
raṅgacchṛṅgoḍḍamaraḍamarūddīpravīṇā pravīṇāḥ

ḍhakkāḍūkkāviraḷamuraḷīkarmaṭhāścābhiyāyuḥ
sphāyaddīpāstamiha mahitoddā mahelā mahelāḥ

Śloka 231

pañchavādyavaravādanāvidhā-
cuñcavo 'asya purataḥ prayāntviha
chatracāmaravidhāriṇo 'bhitaḥ
pṛṣṭato jayajayādivādinaḥ

Tāḷas

The following *tāḷa*s are generally used in Kerala.

1. ***Chempaṭa***: This is the *ādi tāḷa* of 8 *mātrā*s of Carnatic Music. It is referred to as *jhompaṭa* in some old texts which has become *chempaṭa* in Malayalam.
2. ***Pañchāri***: Also mentioned as *pañchakārikā* in some texts. This is equivalent to the *rūpaka tāḷa* of 6 *mātrā*s.
3. ***Aṭanta***: A *tāḷa* of 14 *mātrā*s equivalent to the *aṭa tāḷa*.
4. ***Chempa***: Equivalent of *jhampa* of 10 *mātrā*s.
5. ***Dhruva***: Same as *dhruva tāḷa* of 14 *mātrā*s of Carnatic Music.
6. ***Tripuṭa***: Same as *tiśrajāti tripuṭa* of Carnatic Music of 7 *mātrā*s. This is sometimes called *mu̱ri aṭanta* (that is half of *aṭanta*).
7. ***Eka Tāḷa*** is the same as *eka tāḷa* of Carnatic Music.

There are some other *tāḷa*s known as *lakṣmī tāḷa* (equivalent to *lakṣmīśa tāḷa*), *kuṇṭanāchchi tāḷa, marma tāḷa,* etc. which are found mentioned in some texts, like Oṭṭan Tuḷḷal. But some have gone out of vogue and the details of some of them have become unknown. In folk music they use their own simple but sometimes delightful *tāḷa*s.

The use of the *tāḷa vādyas* in Kerala may be grouped as follows:

1. Those used in temple rituals, tāntric worship, etc.
2. Those used in *sopāna* singing.
3. *Cheṇṭa meḷam* used in temple procession.
4. *Pañchavādyam* used in temple processions, *sevā, ārādhanā, pradakṣiṇā,* etc.
5. *Laya-vinyāsa* on various instruments during temple festivals called *pa<u>rr</u>u tāyampaka,* etc.
6. Instruments used in Kathakali.
7. Oṭṭan Tuḷḷal.
8. Kūṭiyāṭṭam (staging of Sanskrit dramas).
9. Folk music and some rituals of lower caste Hindus like snake worshipping Puḷḷuvans and the Kāḷī worshipping Kuruppu, etc. Ayyappan Pāṭṭu, Veṭṭakkāran (Oru Makan) Pāṭṭu, Antimahākāḷan Pāṭṭu, etc.

Tāntric Worship and Temple Rituals

Instruments used in tāntric worship in temples or playing the *pāṇi* is done for certain *kalaśas, bali,* etc. The instruments used are *pāṇi maram, cheṅgila* and *śaṅkha* and right face of the *cheṇṭa*.

Each beat on the instrument is supposed to coincide with a tāntric action of the priest. Its sound is supposed to represent the unuttered *mantra* embodied in the tāntric sign. As such great importance is attached to have them played properly. Depending on the deity different modes of playing are there like Śaiva Pāṇi, Vaiṣṇava Pāṇi, etc. Each stroke is made at definite time intervals and as the tāntric signs will be made at the same definite intervals, the playing of the instrument and the ritual will go in unison. Many stories and legends are current which will go to show the divinity attached to this but it is a pity that both proper tāntric worship and proper playing have deteriorated. (The extent of deterioration can be imagined by the fact that even temple priests and assistants had struck work in south Kerala). However there is little music nowadays in their playing, though it follows a definite pattern of time measure. Similar daily temple rituals like *pradakṣiṇā, śīveli, śrībhūta bali,* etc. are there, when other instruments like *iṭakka, timila* and *cheṇṭa* are played.

SOPĀNA SINGING

During *pūjā*s (*Prasanna Pūja* done behind closed doors) both in the morning and night, music is sung at the steps leading to the *sanctum sanctorum*. Members of the Mārār (drummer) community do it. Usually *Aṣṭapadi* is sung. The *cheṅgila, iṭakka* and *kuḻittāḷam* are used. The *iṭakka* is the most important instrument and due to the large tonal variation it is a delightful accompaniment. *Iṭakka* has naturally attracted much attention and it deserves to be popularized.

Incidentally, *sopāna* singing is a specialty of Kerala and it is often claimed by many to be a system distinct from Carnatic Music. However, many well-informed persons are of the opinion that it is only a particular regional and functional style of *bāni* of the present Carnatic style. Some rare *rāga*s are found in *sopāna* singing: *ghaṇṭārām, indaḷam, kānakkurīñji, pāṭi,* etc. It is unfortunate that this style has practically died out due to neglect and want of patronage.

Cheṇṭa Meḷam

This is by far the most important and most common assemblage of *tāḷa vādyas*. It is used during elephant (or other) processions for temple festivals. The *cheṇṭa, kompu, kuḻal* and *ilattāḷam* alone are used. The number of each instrument can be many depending on availability of funds and space. The (*utsava vigraha*) deity is brought out and kept on the central one of the caparisoned elephants adorned with tall silk umbrellas, peacock feather fans and *chāmara*. The drums start the *meḷam* and the deity will be taken in procession round the temple in the *prākāram*. The drumming can be in various *tāḷa*s but will usually be in 4 or 5 *kālams* (tempos). Each *kāḷam* will be played according to the time allotted for completing the procession.

The following *meḷams* are played: (1) *pañchāri*, (2) *aṭanta*, (3) *chempa*, (4) *chempaṭa*, (5) *dhruva*, (6) *añchaṭanta*, (7) *pāṇṭi*.

Of these *pañchāri meḷam* is used for processions inside the temple *prākāram* and the *pāṇṭi meḷam* is used for processions outside the temple. The other *meḷams* are all played inside the temple, but they are rarely met with and they are going out of vogue; *chempaṭa* however is played for a short duration before the start of any other *meḷam*.

There is no fixed duration for the *meḷam*. It depends on individual temples or circumstances. A few of the *cheṇṭa*s will be *uruṭṭu cheṇṭa*s which will be played with both hands. They will play the *jātis* or *vinyāsas*. The rest of the *cheṇṭa*s will only keep time.

Taking *pañchāri meḷam* for example, they consider that each leading *cheṇṭa* (*uruṭṭu cheṇṭa*) should be supported by 4 time keeping ones, 3 *ilattāḷam*, 1 *kompu* and 1 *kuḻal*. The leader plays with both hands, the palm alone of the left hand and a stick in the right hand. The assisting *cheṇṭa*s use only one hand with a stick.

The *pañchāri meḷam* is started with the slow tempo of 96 *mātrā*s per *tāḷavaṭṭam*. There is particular *jāti* for the *tāḷavaṭṭam*. The same Jati is repeated in the same manner over and over agaiṇ After three or more *tāḷavaṭṭam*s there will be a *kalāśam* (*muttāyippu* or *mohara*). After that the same *jāti* is repeated. To many people, this endless repetition may be a bit boring, but after one *tāḷavaṭṭam* and a *kalāśam* the tempo is very slightly increased. By slow degrees this tempo is increased — depending on the time. The first stage is played and then the next *kāḷam* of 48 *mātrā*s is taken up. This is also played by repeating the same *jāti*s in the *tāḷavattam* and giving *kalāśam* as in the previous *kāḷam*s. After playing this for some time, the next tempo of 24 *mātrā*s and then that of 12 *mātrā*s and again of 6 *mātrā*s are taken up. When it reaches the 6 *mātrā*s the tempo would be so quick that the connoisseur would find it difficult to keep time by merely nodding the head. His hands will be beating imaginary *cheṇṭa*s in the air. The flourish of the *cheṇṭa*, the *kompu*, *kuḻal* and the *ilattāḷam* and the enthusiasm of the connoisseurs is a sight to see!

One of the top performances of this *meḷam* can be heard at the Kootal Manickam temple at Irinjalakuda and at Perumanam temple, both in Trichur district.

Pañchāri meḷam is considered to be the most aristocratic of the *meḷam*s. Its slow tempo consists of 96 *mātrā*s per *tāḷavaṭṭam* and the leader of the group has to be a really able man to keep track of the *mātrā*s without mistake.

The *pāṇṭi meḷam* is played during procession outside the temples. It is in (*tiśrajāti*) *tripuṭa tāḷa* and is usually played in four stages of 56, 28, 14 and 7 *mātrās*. Here also a fixed *jāti* is played for a number of times and after a certain number of *tāḷavaṭṭams* — there does not seem to be any fixity about it, but is done according to the availability of time — a *kalāśam* is given and again repeated over again. In *pāṇṭi meḷam* however the Jatis played are different for the four *kāḷams* (tempos) unlike the other *meḷam* where the Jati is the same in the slower and faster tempos. One of the best performances of the *pāṇṭi meḷam* can be heard at Trichur Pūram festival. There are mainly two competing parties for this festival and each party will have about 15 leading *cheṇṭas*, some time-keeping *cheṇṭas*, 40 *ilattāḷams*, 24 *kuḻals* and 24 *kompus*. The volume of sound will be so big that it could be heard for miles around.

The *meḷams* are started when the deity is brought out from the temple and is kept on the central decorated elephant. Then the deity does *pradakṣiṇā* of the temple, unless it is taken outside to a maidan or to visit another temple, or for the *paḷḷi veṭṭa* (divine hunting) or for *āṟāṭṭu* (divine bath in the river or sea). It is the usual practice to play the *chempaṭa meḷam* first (that is the *meḷam* in *ādi tāḷa*). This is done for 10 or 15 minutes and then other instruments are played.

For most of the *meḷams*, the slow tempos will be in multiples of 8 of the basic *mātrā* of the *tāḷa*. If it be *pañchāri* (*rūpaka tāḷa*) it will be 6 × 16 = 96 *mātrās* for the first tempo. It it be *chempa*, it will be 10 × 8 = 80 *mātrās*. For *chempaṭa*, 8 × 8 = 64 *mātrās* and so on. The *naṭa* will be usually *chaturaśram* and the *jātis* will be in multiples of 8 *mātrās*. Therefore in the beginning one would feel that all these *meḷams* are being done in the *ādi tāḷa*. Only when the tempo is increased and the *mātrās* reduced to the basic *tāḷa* will it be easily discernible which Tāḷa is being adapted.

CHEMPAṬA MEḶAM

4 *kāḷams,* first stage 64 *mātrā*s eight *chempaṭa vaṭṭams*

AÑCHAṬANTA MEḶAM

4 *kāḷams,* first stage 64 *mātrā*s of eight *chempaṭa vaṭṭams,* but the *jāti* is different from the one used for *chempaṭa meḷam.*

DHRUVA MEḶAM

3 *kāḷams,* first stage 56 *mātrā*s or 7 *chempaṭa vaṭṭams.*

AṬANTA MEḶAM

4 *kāḷams,* first stage 56 *mātrā*s of 7 *chempaṭa vaṭṭam*s but the *jāti*s are different from *dhruva meḷam.*

CHEMPA MEḶAM

5 *kāḷams,* first stage 80 *mātrā*s or 10 *chempaṭa vaṭṭams,* 2nd stage 40 *mātrās,* 3rd 20 *mātrās,* 4th 10 *mātrās,* 5th 5 *mātrā*s.

Some of these *meḷam*s are played for hours together, even up to six hours. During this period, it would be found that the beats of all drums are heard simultaneously, without a false beat. This does credit to the sense of *laya* of these Kerala drummers.

Pañchavādyam

One of the most delightful combinations of *tāḷa vādya*s is the *pañchavādyam* of Kerala. The following instruments are used: *śaṅkha, timila, maddaḷam, kompu, iṭakka* and *ilattāḷam.*

They say that *śaṅkha* is only to give the *oṁkāra nāda* and is not to be considered one of the *vādyams*. There are others who consider *śaṅkha* to be one of the instruments and that *ilattāḷam* is to be considered only as an aid to keep time. It is said that in olden days the *kuḻal* also used to be included in the *pañchavādyam;* anyway, now it is not. *Śuddha maddaḷam* is used now whereas formerly it used to be the more primitive *toppi maddaḷam*. Formerly only one side of the *maddaḷam* used to be played by keeping it in an angular position; now both sides of the *maddaḷam* are played. It was during the time of Sri Venkichan Swami (Venkitachala Iyer) of Thiruvilvamala that some reforms were effected in the *pañchavādyam* playing and the present mode and order were brought about.

The playing starts after the *śaṅkha* is blown three times, the actual start taking place from the middle of the third blow. A full set consists of 7 *timila*, 4 *maddaḷam*, 9 *ilattāḷam*, 7 *kompu*, *iṭakka*, 1 *śaṅkha*. It is played during elephant processions inside the temple and outside, during *dīpārādhana* time, etc.

The *tāḷa* used is *tripuṭa tāḷa* of 7 *mātrā*s. The first slow tempo is in 56 *mātrā*s. Some *jāti*s are repeated for some time and then individual instruments *maddaḷam*, *timila* or *iṭakka* are played individually. This gives much scope for *laya-vinyāsa* and for the artists to show their merit.

The second tempo of 28 *mātrā*s is not elaborated but played for a short time using a special *jāti* for the whole *tāḷavaṭṭam* and the next stage of 14 *mātrā*s is taken up. From this stage the *tripuṭa* character of the *tāḷa* will be noticeable. The next is 7 *mātrā*s and even a faster tempo of 3 *mātrā*s. Finally they close it by playing in *eka tāḷa*. *Timila* alone will be played towards the end. The hands of the *timila* artist would be playing in very quick tempo.

In *pañchavādyam* also according to the availability of time each stage of 56 *mātrā*s to 14 *mātrā*s will be played in increasing tempos, just as one increases the tempo while singing a *nāmāvali* in *bhajana*.

Unlike *cheṇṭa meḷam* where different *tāḷa*s are used, *pañchavādyam* is at present played only in *tripuṭa tāḷa*. There is much scope for research and experimentation in this and attempts should be made to introduce other *meḷam*s also in *pañchavādyam*.

The prominence for these *meḷams*, etc. is only in central Kerala. In south Kerala and north Kerala there is lesser prominence for elephant processions and these *meḷams*. In Trichambaram Temple (Taliparamba, Cannanore district), the deity is taken in procession on the head of the temple priests who dance to some of these *meḷams*.

Laya-Vinyāsa

Laya-vinyāsa on the *cheṇṭa* is known as *tāyampaka* and the *vinyāsa* on other instruments is known as *pa<u>rr</u>u* (*maddaḷa pa<u>rr</u>u, ku<u>l</u>al pa<u>rr</u>u* and *kompu pa<u>rr</u>u*). There is however no *timila pa<u>rr</u>u*.

During temple festivals, *tāyampaka* is done at night. The deity is brought out and kept on a *maṇḍapa* and the drummer starts the *vinyāsa*. The *cheṇṭa* is accompanied by four time-keeping *cheṇṭa*s: two keep time on the left or tension end and two on the right end. Two or three *ilattāḷam*s also accompany. Normally the *vinyāsa* is done in *chempa* (*ādi tāḷa*). After playing for some time in *chaturaśra naṭa* he plays other *naṭa*s also. This is known as *kū<u>r</u>u vāyikkal*: *aṭanta kū<u>r</u>u, pañchāri kū<u>r</u>u, chempa kū<u>r</u>u* when he does *miśra, tiśra* or *khaṇḍa naṭa*s. A performance takes about 1 to 1½ hours.

The *laya-vinyāsa* done on the *maddaḷam* is called *maddaḷa pa<u>rr</u>u*. It is also known as *keḷi* when it is done before the start of Kathakali. A *maddaḷam* is usually accompanied by an *ilattāḷam* only. The *laya-vinyāsa* is on the lines of the *tāyampaka*, but the difference due to the nature of the instrument will of course be there.

Kompu pa<u>rr</u>u is delightful to hear. The *laya-vinyāsa* brought out on a wind instrument is the special feature here. Due to the strenuous nature of the blowing, two or three people take part in it by turns. This also follows the patterns of the other instruments but is of much lesser duration.

Ku<u>l</u>al pa<u>rr</u>u follows a different pattern. While in *cheṇṭa meḷam* the primary function of the *ku<u>l</u>al* is that of a *tāḷa vādya*, in the *pa<u>rr</u>u*, the *ku<u>l</u>al* first plays the *nāṭṭa rāga*. Then some major *rāga* is taken up. After *rāga ālāpa*, a *kīrtana* or *pallavī* is taken up and during the *svaram* singing the *tāḷa-vinyāsa* is brought about. It is accompanied by a *cheṇṭa* and *ilattāḷam*.

Kathakali

Kathakali is the dance drama of Kerala. It is only some 300 years since Kathakali came into being. The actors converse only by sign language with appropriate dancing. Musicians in the background will be singing the *pada*s. The *tāḷa* accompanists play a *cheṅgila, ilattāḷam*, a *maddaḷam* and a *cheṇṭa* if it be a male character who takes the floor. If a female character acts, the *cheṇṭa* will be either absent or will be replaced by an *iṭakka*. All the usual *tāḷa*s are used. In addition to accompanying the singers for the *tāḷa* of the *pada*s the drummers have to play appropriately for the gestures or *mudrā*s shown by the actors. This requires a good skill at adaptation and a thorough knowledge of the technique of Kathakali.

Before the actual beginning of the play there is some times a *meḷappada*.

The *Aṣṭapadi, Mañjutara Kuñjatala* is sung and the Bhāgavatar does a sort of Neraval on the song which is appropriately taken up by the drummers. After that there is a competitive *laya-vinyāsa* by the *maddaḷam* and the *cheṇṭa*. This is a special piece for connoisseurs to appreciate and for the laymen to get thoroughly bored with. The *meḷappada* is done on the *jhampa tāḷa*.

During the acting *kalāśam* is done by the actors. This is a dance representation of the basic sentiment portrayed by the character. Such bits of dancing require special support from the drummers. In one *kalāśa* known as the *aṣṭa kalāśa*, there is a sort of competition between the drummer and the actor. The actor has to dance an appropriate bit to represent the *jati* played by the drummer.

The *tāḷas chempaṭa, chempa, aṭanta, muṟi aṭanta* or *tripuṭa, pañchāri* and *eka tāḷa* are met with in Kathakali. Some of the *śṛṅgāra padas* for love scenes are rendered in very slow tempo. *Aṭanṭa tāḷa* equivalent to *ada tāḷa* of four *kaḷā chaukka* will in effect be a *tāḷa* of *mātrās*. The ease with which a Kathakali artist handles such long-drawn-out *tāḷas* in such a slow tempo would amaze even accomplished artists of Carnatic Music.

Oṭṭan Tuḷḷal

In *oṭṭan tuḷḷal*, stories in verse form are recited showing gestures. Different *tāḷas* are used. The *laya* accompaniments are a *toppi maddaḷam* and a *kuḻittāḷam*. The *toppi maddaḷam* is being replaced by the *mṛdaṅga* now.

Kūṭiyāṭṭam

Kūṭiyāṭṭam is the staging of Sanskrit dramas where *rasa abhinaya* predominates. The characters recite Sanskrit *śloka*s or prose passages from dramas, showing appropriate gestures or *mudrā*s also. For detailing previous events *nirvahaṇam* is performed when only *mudrā*s are shown. There is also a small amount of dancing involved in acting. This as well as the showing of *mudrā*s follows a definite *tāḷa* pattern.

Various *tāḷa*s are used and the *tāḷa vādya*s are the *miḻāvu*, the *iṭakka* and the *kuḻittāḷam*. There are conventions for using certain *tāḷa*s for certain situations, for certain characters and so on. The *miḻāvu*, a pot with its mouth covered with leather, though a primitive sort of instrument is a good one in capable hands.

A *kuḻal* accompaniment is also there for Kūṭiyāṭṭam. Originally this *kuḻal* was to have been a *tāḷa vādya* to play the *jāti*s like the other *tāḷa* instruments but of late it is seen that the artist simply plays *rāga*s or apologies for them according to his whim.

Incidentally, there is an instrument in Tamil Nadu temples known as *kuṭamuḻa* which only goes to show the ties between Tamil Nadu and Kerala. *Miḻāvu* is still in use in Kerala though slowly dying out. An attempt to prevent its decay has already been started by the Kerala Kalamandalam.

Like other old art forms the art of drumming is slowly dying out in Kerala also. While formerly the head of the family used to take particular care to train up boys in the family, such care and the strenuous practice of olden days are absent now. As most boys learn by listening and by following practical demonstrations they know very little of the theory. Even some of the top artists I have approached were unable to explain many points. However those who have undergone some training in classical Carnatic Music were able to explain the salient theoretical aspects of the art. Such people also show a greater tendency to adhere to the theory when they give performances.

There are no books to explain the theory. There are no courses for teaching *cheṇṭa meḷam* in any of the institutions. Some classes are conducted by the Kerala Kalamandalam where the emphasis is of course on the Kathakali aspect of it. They have started a *timila* class for *pañchavādyam*. Their attempt to start a *miḻāvu* class has not succeeded for want of students.

It would be good to write down and publish the *vāyttāri* (*chol-keṭṭu*) of the various *meḷam*s and take recordings from the few elders who are still familiar with them. It is also necessary to bring out a proper textbook on the subject. It is a pity that even the Sangeet Natak Akademi of Kerala has not attempted anything on these lines yet. If the members of the Experts Committee of the Music Academy, Madras will take the initiative in the matter it would be a welcome move.

APPENDIX - C

Oṇa Villu

A SIMPLE quaint instrument of rhythm called *oṇa villu* (ōṇam bow), which was popular once, still survives in the custody of a few enthusiasts. As the name suggests, it is bow shaped. A slat of bamboo or areca or "elephant" palm wood is bent like a small bow and a pencil thin bamboo rod is fixed in the position of a bow string. A pencil size wooden rod for striking the "string" (rod) completes the instrument. It is held by the left hand across the chest. It is played by striking the "bow string — rod" with the pencil size rod held in the right hand. This produces a twang like sound the pitch of which can be altered by exerting pressure to slightly bend the bow by the left shoulder and left hand. The variation in the pitch produces different tones and this variation in the tones is used to play rhythm on the instrument. All the *jāti*s (*bol*s — *Eṇṇaṅgaḷ*) required to play a *tani āvarttanam* or *laya-vinyāsam* or *ṭāyampaka* can be played. A regular *tāyampaka* as is done on a *cheṇṭa* can be performed with it. It used to be very popular.

Time was when many youngsters got trained on this. It is not only a good pastime but also an art. What is important is that the youngsters are given a proper insight and grounding in the art and science of *tāḷam*. It used to be widely played during the *oṇam* time. There are still a few masters — mostly *cheṇṭa* players — who can give a classical performance on it. The simplicity of its construction and the free availability and cheapness of the materials of construction makes it ideal for teaching children. If only folk-lore enthusiasts, Yuvak-Kendras and Art Associations take it up earnestly many children can easily be trained.

There is a folk performance, especially in Trichur area, called Kummāṭṭi Kaḷi. One or more artists — usually boys — are attired by covering their body with a medicinal plant called *kummāṭṭi pullu*. Sometimes dry banana leaves are also used. The face is covered with different masks — a demon, a monkey, an old lady and so on. They jump about and dance to the songs sung by their friends. *Oṇa villu* is the main instrument for rhythmic support. A number of limericks — nonsensical verses — are sung for this. Merry-making seems to be the only aim.

> *A sage performed a Homa long ago*
> *In the* homa kuṇḍa *a stone sprouted*
> *On top of the stone a* pīṭham *was born*
> *On the* pīṭham *a sword appeared*
> *He took up the sword and roared*
> *He called out Kāḷī O Kāḷī*
> *Kāṭan Kāḷī (Bhadrakāḷī) answered his call*
> *He went over to Kodungallur*
> *He went round the temple thrice*
> etc. etc. etc.

Another song:

> *What is it Rāvaṇa, why is it Rāvaṇa*
> *The reason for your stealing Sīta*
> *Was it your own idea, or*
> *Did someone ask you to do it?*
> *It was my own idea*

I was not advised by any

etc. etc. etc.

Kummāṭṭi Kaḷi is an annual feature during *oṇam* season in some temples. The elders of different localities arrange for it on the third day of *oṇam*. They first perform in front of the temple and then go about performing it from house to house collecting pocket money. *Oṇam* is a time for merry making and enjoying.

An instrument called *villu* is used in the performance of *villu pāṭṭu* in the southern areas of Kerala and Tamil Nadu. That instrument — bow-shaped — is big and on its fibre string, bells and jingles are suspended. The jingling produced by beating the strings used to keep time for story telling in that art form.

APPENDIX - D

Bhagavatī Pāṭṭu of the Maṇṇāns

MAṆṆĀN is a community belonging to the Harijan section in Kerala. Their main jobs are laundering and acting as "priests" in the worship of Bhagavatī and some minor deities. While they are washermen of the lower castes, for clothes that are ritually unclean (after women's menses, after childbirth, and after death), the Maṇṇātti (female of the Maṇṇān) has to wash them even for the highest castes like Nampūtiris; only then will such clothes become ritually pure.

Velan and Perumaṇṇān are two castes allied to the Maṇṇāns. The Maṇṇāns draw powder pictures (*kaḷam*) representing Kāḷī or Bhagavatī and some minor deities like Kuṭṭichāttan, Muṇṭiyan, etc. do *pūjā* to the deity invoked in the *kaḷam*, and sing songs in praise of them (Tōṟṟam Pāṭṭu). They can hardly be called songs, only a few notes are used, and it may be more appropriate to term them as chants. They are however strong in rhythm. Muṇṭiyan Pāṭṭu is performed for the welfare of cattle and agricultural activities. Strangely, one portion of the Muṇṭiyan Pāṭṭu describes the building of Kūttambalam (temple theatre) for the performance of Kūṭṭu and Kūṭiyāṭṭam.

According to their myth, Chāttan is the son of Lord Śiva in a tribal woman. As Chāttan is said to be diminutive in size, he is referred as Kuṭṭichāttan (Kuṭṭi, i.e. boy or small). The word *chāttan* is also said to be derived from *śāstā*. This goblin-like demi-god is said to help or trouble people according to the way he is worshipped. Trichur is reputed to be a centre for Chāttan worship and people irrespective of caste or religion make offerings to him. KuṭṭiChāttan can be induced to do harm to one's enemies. Doing *pūjā* to KuṭṭiChāttan is considered by many as equivalent to black magic. One important activity of the Maṇṇāns is to draw powder pictures of Chāttan, do *pūjā* and sing songs. As accompaniment for this, they use only some drums like *cheṇṭa, tuṭi* and *īl̲ar̲a* (a brum-brum sound is heard from this when the skin is rubbed with a curved stick).

The most important priestly activity of the Maṇṇāns is to draw designs or pictures with coloured powders representing Bhagavatī, do *pūjā* to it, and sing songs praising her and describing her exploits. These songs are called Bhagavatī Pāṭṭu. The various designs drawn have varied esoteric significance. The repertoire of these songs is pretty large, and it will take several nights to complete one round of it. This ritual is normally done in Kāvus (grove temples) and in the houses of Īl̲avas and other lower caste people. During the ritual, a person may be possessed and give oracular predictions. During the *pūjā* they may make offerings of arrack (liquor) and blood (by cutting the neck of a cock and spilling a few drops of blood) as *naivedya*.

In the singing of these songs, the singers accompany themselves on a simple but quaint stringed instrument called *nantuṇi*. *Nantuṇi* has a rectangular hollow body of wood with a tail that projects at an angle. Strings made of sisal or palm fibre are stretched over the body, tied to an iron hook at the top end and tightened to a peg at the bottom. A small wooden bridge is also provided. Five frets are fixed over the resonator. The instrument is about 4½ feet long and 6 inches wide. The resonator will be about 14 inches. The strings are strummed by a small buffalo-horn plectrum. One string is slightly thicker and is used as a drone. By pressing the thinner wire on the frets, different notes can be produced. Though the five frets would remind us of the old pentatonic scale, the Maṇṇāns produce only a couple of notes and it is used for the rhythm. It is normally held in the vertical position on the left shoulder and the left-hand fingers press on the frets and the right hand strums.

The projection of the tail at the end is at an angle. This seems to indicate that the instrument might have been developed from a harp or *yāḻ* (Tamil, Malayalam). This idea is strengthened in Malayalam poetry referring these songs as Vyāḻan Pāṭṭu. The word *vyāḻan* might have been used in the sense of *yāḻam* (pertaining to a *yāḻ* as harps were called in the old language). Hence it may not be wrong to think that *nantuṇi* is the first stage in the development of the fretted *vīṇā* from the harp.

Before beginning their songs, they refer to the instrument, *nantuṇi*, as a divine child. The *nantuṇi* is kept on the divine lap. An approximate gist of their description is like this:

O Nantuṇi, what is your divine name,
Come my daughter,
The goddess of Kuṟumba,
Tell us your name and your greatness and sing.

The description goes on in this fashion. The *bilva* (*bela*) tree in the mountain is cut. It is shaped by the wind, the inside is scooped out with a chisel and its two parts are

Śakti and Śiva. Various gods are installed on the body, and Bhadrakāḷī resides in the centre. The two strings are *anna* and *ālamba*. When strummed by the right hand with the left hand pressing on the strings, the two birds sitting on the tree will chirp — O! come to see and hear it.

There is one more community in Kerala who draw *kaḷam* of Bhagavatī and sing in her praise. They are *kuṟup*s — a section of the Nair community. They do the ritual even in the houses of Nampūtiri brāhmins. They normally sing about the exploits of Bhagavatī, like the stories in *Devī Māhātmya (Durgāsaptaśatī)*, the killing of the demon Dārika, etc. They also use the *nantuṇi*. In some of the Devī temples, the *kuṟup*s sing these songs as a daily service. The Thirumandham Kunnu Devī temple in Malappuram district is a famous centre for this. These songs are called Tōṟṟam songs. The word *tōṟṟam* is used in the sense of a picture.

Among the songs rendered by the Maṇṇāns, one of the most lengthy is the one related to the story of the anklet. The ritual takes several days to complete. The story looks like a folk version of the famous story, chilampu (anklet), dealt with in the Tamil classic *Śilappadikāram*. It must be remembered that *Śilappadikāram* was written in Kerala by Ilango, a brother of the Cera king Cenguṭṭuvan. *Śilappadikāram* is a celebrated classic in Tamil and contains a wealth of information on various art forms like music, dance, etc. Whether this folk version sung by the Maṇṇāns came first or whether the classical version in *Śilappadikāram* came first is a moot point. Only the main points in the two versions are the same. Instead of Kaṇṇaki and Kovalan in the Tamil classic, the Maṇṇāns refer to them as Deviyāḷ (Devī goddess) and Pālakan. It is composed in a mixture of songs and narratives (Pāṭṭu and Chollu-mo̱li).

In the story, when the couple find that they have lost all their wealth, the divine anklet of Deviyāḷ is taken by Pālakan for sale in the Pāṇḍian capital. He is however cheated by the royal goldsmith and accused of stealing the anklet of the queen. The Pāṇḍian king sentences Pālakan to death by impaling. Deviyāḷ sees some bad omens and goes in search of her husband. Finding him impaled, she becomes possessed and destroys the Pāṇḍian King and the goldsmith. Finally she installs the soul of Pālakan in a temple as also her own soul and goes into eternal meditation.

One would be amazed at the wonderful imagery and forceful expression found in these songs sung by the Maṇṇāns. A couple of examples are given below. Pālakan goes to the capital of Pāṇḍian kingdom to sell the anklet of gold (*chilampu*) given by his wife Deviyāḷ As she receives no information about Pālakan even after a week and as she sees some bad omens, she starts in search of her husband, seeking information from various living beings on the way.

Seeing a jackfruit tree on the way, she asks "O jack tree (*pḷāmaram*), have you seen my husband going this way? Did you hear the jingling of my anklets which he had taken for selling?" At this, a branch of the tree breaks off and falls down and latex starts trickling down from it. Seeing this the Devī remarks, Your mind is sorrowful and agitated, and you weep like me. You have my blessings. May you bear a lot of fruits. May the fruits be used for making curry and jackfruit *pāyasam* (pudding), and served to all during marriages in the neighbourhood. When you grow old, may your trunk be cut down and an idol of the goddess be made out of the heartwood and may *pūjā* be done to you daily.

Further, when the Deviyāḷ goes on her way, she comes across a cow. She asks the cow if it had seen her husband or heard the jingling of her anklet. The cow tries to butt her with its horns and stamp her with its front legs. The Devī is angered and says,

> When I am agitated and seek information, you are trying to attack me. May your horns and hooves get decayed and worm-infested and when you die, may a Pariah take you, suspended by your legs on a bamboo pole. May he cut open your stomach and take out your skin. May he cure it and fix it on a drum so that you get beaten up over and over again even after you die.

Another person she met on her journey was a young damsel, who was standing near a well with her friends. When the Devī enquired about her husband, the girl laughed clapping her hands and said,

> Here is a woman enquiring about her husband. Does the water pot go in search of the well or does the well go in search of a water pot? Does a flower go in search of a bee or the bee in search of the flower? It is the male who should go in search of the female. What is the world coming to that a woman goes in search of a man?

The Devī got very angry and cursed her:

> Not understanding the agony of my heart and sympathizing with me, you are clapping your hands and laughing. I shall give you a 'boon.' May you get married soon. May your husband go for a hunt. May he get killed in the forest by a tiger. May his friends bring his dead body and lower it in a grave. May the *tāli* (marriage badge) you wear on your neck be

> snatched away and placed on the face of your dead husband. And then, when you weep and cry beating your chest with those very hands that you are clapping with now, you will understand the sorrow and agony of my heart.

Can the depth of her agony be brought about in a more forceful way? Folk songs contain such a wealth of ideas and poetic expressions. The text of the entire ritual has not been printed, only part of it has been published. The song, etc. have not been recorded in full. The highbrows who neglect such folk literature know not what they are missing.

APPENDIX - E

The Puḷḷuvans and their Music

WHILE the worship of snakes is found spread throughout India, it is raised to the level of a fine art in Kerala. A caste known as the Puḷḷuvans is specially associated with serpent worship. The rituals adopted by the Puḷḷuvans consist of the following:

1. A very artistic picture of the holy serpents is drawn on the ground with coloured powders.
2. The divine presence of the holy serpents is invoked on it and *pūjā* is offered.
3. Songs on the origin of the serpents and in praise of them are sung to the accompaniment of two instruments, the *puḷḷuvan vīṇā* and the *puḷḷuvan kuṭam*.
4. A ritual dance with a lighted wick is done called *tiri uḻiccal*.
5. Two young girls are made to sit on the drawing, and they get "possessed" with divine serpents, and give oracular predictions.[1]

---

1. The ritual is known as *pāmpin kaḷam* in some areas. In Kerala, similar rituals of drawing pictures and singing songs and a person getting possessed, etc. are there for other deities like Bhadrakāḷī, Kirāta Mūrti, etc. The songs are known as Tōṟṟam Pāṭṭu. In South Kanara a similar ritual for Holy Serpents known as Nāga Maṇḍala is prevalent. A comparative study is not however attempted here.

While our main concern here is with the music and musical instruments of the Puḷḷuvans, we shall briefly examine their background before we consider the subject proper.

The Puḷḷuvans belong to the old classification of untouchables among the Hindus in Kerala. It is a very small community and is still classified as a backward one. Unlike many other communities in Kerala, they follow the patrilenial system. Polyandry was prevalent among them in former days. They do not usually work as agricultural or other labourers. Their main source of livelihood is their cult of snake worship. They are usually found to have a good voice.

In most ancestral houses of Hindus in Kerala, a *pratiṣṭhā* — a ritual seat — for the Divine Serpents would be found called Sarpakkāvu.[2] A small masonry platform is raised on the ground in the compound and stone images of hooded serpents called *chitrakūṭam* are installed on the top. Oil lamps are lighted at this place daily at dusk by way of worship. No one, who is in pollution or ritually unclean, goes near the place. *Pūjā*s are done on special days, at least once a year. In some houses, a brāhmin priest conducts it, in others the Puḷḷuvans do it. Only when an elaborate *pūjā* is required do they draw the picture of the serpents and go through the detailed rituals mentioned earlier.

The word *puḷḷuvan* is said to be derived from *puḷḷu* which means a bird. There is a belief that there are some evil spirits which take the form of birds and fly at dusk and that their

2. *Nāga pratiṣṭhā* is seen at the foot of baniyan trees in temple compounds, where the public can worship. But the Sarpakkāvu here relates to the ones found in private houses.

appearance cause sickness to infants and children.[3] The Pulluvans do some *pūjā* to exorcize the evil spirits from infants. The exorcism is still practised by them. The Pulluvans also sing special song to ward off the "Evil Eye" or "Evil Tongue." Such songs are called "Nāveru Pāṭṭu."[4]

During the lean months — July, August (Karkaṭaka month) — when there are no agricultural operations due to heavy rains in Kerala and also during the comparatively prosperous months after the harvests, the Pulluvans can be seen going from house to house and singing songs on the serpents, and eke out their livelihood from the presents obtained during such "singing" trips. Their major income however comes from the elaborate rituals conducted annually in some houses.

This form of snake worship is known as *pāmpin kaḷam.* A suitable place is selected in the courtyard of the house

3. There is a common belief that those born under the star Kēṭṭa are more prone to the sinister influence of the bird Pullu.

4. Different rituals are found in various communities to ward off the "Evil Eye" and "Evil Tongue," but the Pulluvans have made a fine art of it. After singing the Naveru sometimes they sing what is known as Manjal Mūḷikkuka (the humming of the palanquin-bearers) as an entertainment. At the end of it the Pulluvan *does* a conversation with his *vīṇā*, a subtle method to wangle more presents from the householder:

   Pulluvan: O *vīṇā*, "what did they say?"

   Vīṇā: They said "We shall give, We shall give"

   Pulluvan: "What if they do not give?"

   Vīṇā: "O Shame, O Shame, O Shame"

   The Pulluvans claim they have the blessings of sage Nārada and hence their ability to ward off the evils.

and a small *pantal* is erected about 7 or 8 ft square. The ground is well prepared and made firm and smooth by smearing with cowdung. On this level ground a drawing called *kaḷam* — a *raṅgolī* — is drawn depicting a picture of intertwined serpents with their hoods spread at the middle of the four sides of a square. They use five coloured powders, white (rice powder), yellow (turmeric), red (*kumkumam*), green (powdered dry leaves), and black (powdered rice husk charcoal). Excepting for a very few instruments like a straight edge, it is all free hand drawing. Some decorative work however is done with perforated powder droppers (*kōlakkuḻal*). In some places, the picture of *nāga yakṣī*, a semi human-cum-serpent form is also drawn. This is supposed to represent Kadru, the mother of the serpents in the Purāṇas. There are a few places where these drawings are done on huge dimensions covering several square yards.

The *pantal* is gaily decorated with tender coconut leaf and mango leaf *tōraṇams*, flower garlands, etc. On this *raṅgolī* are kept a measure of paddy, rice, *aval*, fruits, water in a *kiṇṭi*, coconuts, tender coconuts, jaggery, flowers, a mirror (*vāl kaṇṇaṭi*), lighted lamps, etc. With a winnow (*muṟam*), the *pūjarī* (not necessarily the Puḷḷuvan) goes round the drawing requesting Garuḍa, the sworn enemy and cousin of the serpents, not to come anywhere near, lest the serpents get afraid to visit the place. The family members, the girls who are to be possessed by the snakes, and the Puḷḷuvans go to the Sarpakkāvu in the compound ceremonially escorted by young girls doing *tālappoli* (holding a plate containing flowers, rice, a half coconut with a wick-burning oil in it). *Pūjā* is done at the Sarpakkāvu and after requesting the serpents to take their seat in the drawing the party return to the *pantal*. Special *pūjā*s are done for the Trinity, the serpents, the *aṣṭa vasus*, etc. A portion of the offerings and a lighted wick are taken and kept outside the drawing and are intended for non-poisonous snakes said to be the offspring of one of the holy snakes who lost all power due to a curse from the mother for disobedience. At the end of the *pūjā*, one of the Pulluvans will take in his hand a bunch of burning wicks held inside plantain stem cuttings. He will go round the drawing dancing and waving the flame and even pass the flame all over his body. This acrobatic dance is done to the accompaniment of cymbals keeping the rhythm. This is a form of *dīpārādhana* and is known as *tiri uliccal*.[5]

To the accompaniment of their *vīṇā, kuṭam* and *tāḷam* (big cymbals) the Pulluvans — male and female — start singing the praise of the holy snakes Anantan, Vāsuki, Mahā Padman, Śaṅkhuvālan, Nahuṣan, Kāḷian, Airāvatan, Piṅgalan, Hemaguhan, Manimudgaran, Dadhimukhan, etc.

A couple of young girls — usually pre-puberty ones — bathed and wearing traditional dress and made ritually pure are made to sit on the drawing. They hold a bunch of areca flowers in their hands. Their hair is untied and hung loose. The Pulluvans sing their songs with gusto and the tempo and the volume are increased appropriately. In most cases, before long the girls go into a trance, and get "possessed" by the divine serpents. They drag themselves all over the drawing. The Pulluvans ask the girls who they are. They start swaying their heads. They reply they are

5. Of late this Tiri Uliccal is seen performed during the worship of other deities like Ayyappan.

Maṇi Nāga, or Kari Nāga or Nāga Yakṣī as the case may be. They are then asked if they are satisfied with the *pūjā* and worship. If the answer is yes, then their blessings are invoked on the household. If the answer happens to show some dissatisfaction, the householder promises to do whatever is demanded. The girls then swoon. They are removed and they recover after some time.

A fresh drawing is again made and the stories connected with the snakes from the *Mahābhārata* are sung till day break. If the possessed girls say that they are not satisfied then the ritual will have to be repeated again the next day and the day after. There have been instances where negative answers were received for several days at a stretch. Then the astrologers were consulted who divined that some un-worshipped *nāga pratiṣṭhā* (Sarpakkāvu) exists in the possession of the householder or that he has not fulfilled some previous promise to the serpents, etc. When these are done the answer "satisfied" is obtained from the girls at the very next session.

The stories sung from the *Mahābhārata* relate to the portion about the sage Kaśyapa; his two wives Kadru and Vinatā; the birth of 1008 snake sons to Kadru; the bet between Kadru and Vinatā, and the victory of the former by trickery; Vinatā becoming a servant maid of Kadru; the birth of Aruṇa and Garuḍa; Garuḍa bringing *amṛta;* his fight with his cousins; the story of the death of Parīkṣit by the bite of Takṣaka; Janamejaya, the son of Parīkṣit doing a sacrifice of the serpents; Kṛṣṇa and Kāḷiya; the penance of Ananta and his becoming the bed of Mahāviṣṇu, etc. The repertoire is long enough to sing the whole night, say from 9 p.m. to 5 a.m. The texts of these songs are of unknown authorship. In some areas, the *Mahābhāratam Kiḷippāṭṭu* of

Tuñcat Eḻuttacchan (known as the Ādi Kavi of Malayalam language) is used. One Panikkalathor Kannan Nair of Varavoor village (Trichur district) is also said to have composed these songs. The compositions are in the Kiḷippāṭṭu style of Malayalam poetry. One of their songs contains an interesting story of the origin of the Puḷḷuvans. During the burning of Khāṇḍava forest by Agni with the help of Arjuna, one snake escaped half burnt from the forest. One girl fetching water in a mud pot saw the burning snake and extinguished the fire with the water and kept the pot on the ground. The snake slid into the pot and remained there. The girl offered *pūjā* to the pot for some days. The pot turned into an ant hill (supposed natural residence of the snakes). The snake was pleased and gave a boon to the girl saying, "I am pleased with your worship. You and your children and theirs in turn continue to worship the snakes. We shall always make our divine presence felt whenever you invoke us by singing our praise to the strumming of the Pot instrument." The Puḷḷuvans are said to be the offspring of this girl and the pot instrument is used in memory of the pot that was refuge of the snake which escaped from the forest fire.[6]

There are regional differences in the songs and the rituals.[7] One subsect is called Pāṇa Puḷḷuvan who are found

---

6. There are different versions about the community to which the girl originally belonged, though there is agreement that she belonged to a higher caste. Why and how the descendents of the girl happened to be relegated to a very low caste is not clear.

7. As is the case with most other art forms there are much regional variations in Kerala. The names of communities connected with the same type of art or ritual vary. The texts →

in Pālghāṭ district. They use only the pot instrument but not the *vīṇā*. One important centre for snake worship is Mannarasala near Alleppey, where the divine seat for the serpents is in the basement (Nilavarakkuṇṭu) in a Nambūtiri brāhmin's house. Puḷḷuvans from many places assemble there for festivals. Another important place is the Pampumekkavu Mana in Trichur district. In Kerala the fear of offending the serpent is so deep that even non-Hindus take the help of a Hindu priest to ritually remove the old Sarpakkāvus from newly purchased property.[8]

We shall consider their two instruments:

Puḷḷuvan Vīṇā

This is a fiddle-like instrument.[9] It has a dish-shaped resonator called Kiṇṇam about 8 inch diameter and 3½ inch depth, made of a light wood (usually *kumkumam* tree). Attached to this is a tapering stem of harder wood like jack or teak 12 inch long at the end of which is fixed a peg (*śaṅkupiri*). The face of the resonator dish is covered with the skin of monitor lizard (*uṭumbu tōl*). Only one string is there and is made of the twisted fibre of a medicinal creeper called *nāga chittamṛtu*.[10] The bow is about two feet long and

→ of the songs of the same community for the same art form vary. What is related here is what is normally found in Trichur district, which is in central Kerala and is often described as the cultural centre of Kerala.

8. In the recent past, there was a theft from the Mannarasala temple. The thief (a non-Hindu) was caught a few days after from a hotel where he made a commotion one night saying that a cobra has been visiting his room every night and it was about to attack him.

9. It is called *vīṇā kuñju* (small *vīṇā*) in some areas.

10. Tinosopara Cordifolia, known as guḍūcī in Sanskrit.

is made from the wood of the arecanut palm. The bow strings are also made from the above-said creeper. At the end of the bow, two round metal jingles are inserted. These are sounded by the to and fro movements of the bow and this keeps the rhythm for the songs. The tension of the bow string is altered by the little finger of the right hand between the strings and the bow while holding it. The latex from a cactus was being used to smear on the strings but now only rosin is used.

The lizard skin covering the dish is not only pasted on the wood but its edges are strung with threads which are tightened on to a loop of cotton thread at the bottom middle of the resonator. A small triangular piece of wood is used as a bridge and is kept above the middle of the skin covering the resonator. Only one string is used and this starts from a nail fixed at the top of the resonator and the other end fixed to the screw peg and tightened. As only one string is used only four or five notes are produced. While the *vīṇā* does not accompany the music of the songs in full it acts as a *śruti* and *tāḷa* accompaniment and also keeps up the refrain.

Puḷḷuvan Kuṭam

This is a sphere-shaped mud pot of the type used in villages to carry water, but is much stronger than the normal water pot. Two sizes are found — one of about 30 litre capacity which is normally used by males for the rituals and another about half this capacity which is used by the females when they go on their singing tours. A circular hole about 4 inch is made at the bottom of the pot. About half to three fourths of the pot is covered with calf skin from the bottom up and it is pasted on to the pot. The edges of the skin are strung with thin leather thongs which are braced and tightened to a loop of leather fixed below the neck of the pot. Two thin leather thongs about 27 inches are twisted together and passed through a small hole in the leather covering the hole made in the bottom of the pot. A knot at the end of the thongs prevents it from slipping through. The free end of the twisted thong is fixed to a small bamboo tube. A 27-inch long wooden slat is kept on the ground and held firm by the thigh of the artist sitting on it. The pot is kept over the left thigh with its mouth facing left and it is held with the left arm embracing it. The bamboo tube with the leather string attached to it is fixed on the right end of the slat, by inserting the tube into the slat. The pot is moved sufficiently to the left to keep the thong taut, and when it is plucked by a plectrum of horn or hard wood piece kept on the right hand, a *brum brum* sound is heard. The palm of the left hand is made to rest on the slat and the index finger is used to stop the vibration of the thong for pauses required during the rhythm. The instrument is mainly used for *tāḷa*. By altering the tension on the thongs by the upper arm embracing the pot, tonal variations are obtained and it can even be used as an instrument for *śruti*. The tonal variations obtained make it suitable as a good *tāḷa* instrument, and the Puḷḷuvans play a Tani Āvarttanam on it and call it *tāyampaka*.[11] The following *tālas* are used in the songs of the Puḷḷuvans.

Muttāḷam — 5 *mātrās*

Nālām tāḷam — 4 *mātrās*

11. *Tāyampaka* is usually used to denote a *tani āvarttanam* on the *cheṇṭa*, but such solo demonstration of *tāḷas* on other instruments is also at times called *tāyampaka*. See the author's article in the *Journal of Madras Music Academy*, vol. XXXVIII, 1967, pp. 83-102.

Pañchāri — 5 *mātrās*

Tripuṭa — 7 *mātrās*

Chempa — 10 *mātrās*

Añchaṭanta[12] — 16 *mātrās*

In the songs sung by the Puḷḷuvans the outlines or major phrases of the following *rāgas* can be heard : (1) *saurāṣṭram*, (2) *śrīrāgam*, (3) *madhyamāvati*, (4) *toḍi*, (5) *sāveri*, (6) *kalyāṇi*, (7) *edukulakāmbhoji*, (8) *chenchuruṭṭi*, and (9) *ghaṇṭāram* (of Kathakali music).

In the palm-leaf manuscripts and note books with these artists, the names of several *rāgas*, like śaṅkarābharaṇam, kāmbhoji, etc. are seen, but I have not been able to come across any Puḷḷuvan who is capable of identifying *rāgas*. They only sing in the traditional manner they have learnt it. During an interview, a very old Puḷḷuvan remarked to me that according to tradition only four *rāgas* are prescribed for the Puḷḷuvans: *saurāṣṭram, madhyamāvati, śrīrāgam* and *ghaṇṭāram*. He was however not able to identify the *rāgas* while he sang.

Much work remains to be done in analysing the *rāgas* sung, in determining the influence of the *rāgas* and the instruments, in the girls getting *possessed*, etc. Alas, the pernicious influence of the film music has started rearing its ugly head even in the rendering of some of the Puḷḷuvans. As in the case of other traditional art forms, the younger generation is unable to follow the Kula To̱ḻil and it is high time that proper recordings are taken to preserve what is left of this fine art form and efforts made to sustain it.

---

12. See the author's article on *kombu vādya* in the *Journal of Madras Music Academy*, vol. XLIV, 1973, pp. 170-77, for details of *añchaṭanta tāḷa*.

Afterword

The Editors' Reflections on L.S. Rajagopalan's Essays on Temple Musical Instruments of Kerala

These essays of Shri L.S. Rajagopalan (LSR) on Temple Musical Instruments of Kerala, published during the period 1967 to 2005 in the *Journal of the Madras Music Academy*, *Sangeet Natak* and others are a treasure of information on traditions, legends, tales and anecdotes, specifications, musicology, etc.

Based on his general survey, LSR brings out a basic difference between north and south Indian music. While the north Indian music emphasizes melody, the south Indian Music emphasizes rhythm and "when it comes to Kerala, rhythm completely overshadows melody."

A divine world of rhythm is unveiled through these essays. LSR brings out the intimate relations of sound with rituals using quotes from *Tantrasamuccaya* along with *śloka*s and passages from authoritative Sanskrit works such as *Nāṭyaśāstra, Saṅgīta Ratnākara, Saṅgīta Makaranda, Sangīta Dāmodara*, etc. For example, a whole lot of initiation rituals are prescribed for *miḻavu*. When a *miḻavu* become unusable elaborate rituals are prescribed for its *saṁskāra* (burial). The invocation, *mṛtyum jaya hara hara śambho,* is the *tāḷa* (*tripuṭa tāḷa* of 7 *mātrā*s) for playing *timila*. Each beat on *pāṇi maram* and *cheṅgila* is supposed to coincide with a *tāntric mantra. Sopāna saṅgīta,* a specialty of Kerala is intimately connected with *iṭakka* which is hung from a peg or rafter. And thereby hangs a tale of Lord Viṣṇu and Lord Śiva. Vindhyāvāsinī (Bhagavatī, Lord Kṛṣṇa's sister) is the *devatā* of *iṭakka*. Śiva is present on the right side and Umā is present on the left of *maddaḷam* and the sound from the *maddaḷam* is divine. The rituals performed by the *maddaḷam* artist before *araṅgu keḷi* for Kathakali [same rituals are performed for Kṛṣṇāṭṭam (at Guruvayur) also] are meant to invoke the divine world of *Nāda-Brahman*.

LSR draws references from the Sanskrit epic, *Mahābhārata*, the Tamil classic *Śilappadikāram*, old Malayalam works such as *Uṇṇunīli Sandeśam, Chandrotsavam, Rāmakatha Pāṭṭu, Mahābhāratam Kiḷippāṭṭu* (Malayalam retelling of *Mahābhārata*) and Oṭṭan Tuḷḷal works (Kuñchan Nambiar). LSR points out: "Other such references should be the subject of research as they would give some guidelines for the study of musical instruments." LSR wants the enthusiasts to pick up this and proceed further.

Occasionally the reader gets some glimpses of the society. In his essay on *ilattāḷam*, LSR mentions the artists playing in the temple of *mahārājā* of Cochin at Tripunithura (to get a few days food and wages) using dummy *ilattāḷam*s cut out from arecanut flower sheath (*pāḷa*), since they were too poor to afford the real instruments made of bell metal. The unknown artist from Bījāpur, playing with *kartāl*s (a pair of hemispherical cymbals) made of cast iron, producing all the *bol*s of *tabala*, amazing many veteran players of *mṛdaṅga* and musicians is another incident.

LSR indicates several stories and anecdotes. The anecdote of Ṣaṭkāla Govinda Mārār [*ṣaṭkāla* (six periods) so called since he had the rare expertise of singing *pallavī* in six *kāla*s supported by his instrument *tamburu* having 7 strings] being instrumental in Saint Tyāgarāja singing his famous composition, "Entaro Mahānubhāvulu" [according to Ullur, (*Kerala Sāhitya Charitram*, vol. 4, page 9)] took place in M.E. 1023 (CE 1837).

On specifications, see where LSR's observations can lead us to: On *iṭakka* he writes about four wooden pegs (*jīva*s) inserted between ropes holding the rings: sixteen multi-coloured balls are hung from each *jīva kōl*, probably representing the 64 arts!

Discussing on the tradition of *aṣṭapadi* singing, LSR notes that the *rāga*s used in Kerala for singing *aṣṭapadi* are not always those prescribed in the texts. Another significant observation is that, in Kerala, *aṣṭapadi* is sung not only in the temples of Viṣṇu, but also in Śiva, Bhagavatī and Śāsta temples and specified *rāga*s should be used for different periods of the day! LSR further appeals to the music experts to try to salvage the old *rāga*s such as *naḷatta, śrīkaṇṭhi, pūvāḷi, sāmanta malahari* in which *tyāṇi*s were sung earlier.

LSR indicates the history and origins of *pañchavādyam* (orchestra of *timila, maddaḷam, iṭakka, kompu, ilattāḷam* and *śaṅkha*) through the efforts of Venkichan Swamy and Madhava Warrier in the 1920s.

From the use of *tiśrajāti tripuṭa*, the use of *rakti rāga*s and the use of some of the *śṛṅgāra padam*s for *iṭakka pradakṣiṇam* LSR suggests that at one time, there might have been the dancing of women preceding the deity. He quotes a *śloka* from *Tantrasamuccaya* to support this point. Presenting a complete picture of music and dance for worship, LSR gives the full text of the *padam, Kāmini Maṇi* composed by Swati Tirunal (along with English translation) used for Mohinī Āṭṭam and for rendering in *kurum kuḻal* in temples.

Yes, we find that these musical instruments are closely related to temple worship. For example, *pañchāri meḷam* is used for processions inside the temple and *pāṇḍi meḷam* is used for processions outside the temple.

LSR draws our attention to non-temple related instruments as well. He states that the wooden water drawing pulley is familiar to Keralites and regrets that they have not chosen to develop a *kastatarang*. Considering the martial tradition, LSR wonders whether the Indian Army will adopt *kompu* in place of the bugle. The toy *pīppi* made from coconut palm leaf by children is also noted by LSR.

LSR notes the simplicity of *Oṇa Villu* construction and the free availability and cheapness of the material of construction. Simultaneously, he points out that all the *jāti*s required to play a *tani āvarttanam* or *laya-vinyāsa* or *tāyampaka* can be played by experts on this simple quaint instrument of rhythm. LSR enriches his essay adding the translations of two limericks — nonsensical verses which are sung with the rhythmic support of *Oṇa Villu*.

Way back in 1974, LSR opined that the time was already overdue for the establishment of an institution for the teaching, preservation and research in musical instruments. In 2009 can we say better late than never?

L.S. Rajagopalan:

A Brief Life Sketch

L.S. Rajagopalan was born on 9 November 1922 at Kunnamkulam in central Kerala, the youngest son of L.S. Subbaraya Iyer and Lakshmi Ammal. His father was employed in the educational service of Cochin State as Headmaster of government high schools, and was Inspector of Schools when he retired from the service. Rajagopalan had four elder brothers and four sisters; the youngest alone is alive today.

Since his childhood, Rajagopalan's parents had encouraged him in music. He used to listen in to the music classes of his sisters and nieces, and his father would explain to him the scientific aspects of Carnatic music. Rajagopalan studied up to the intermediate class at St Thomas College, Trichur (1937-39), and then moved to Bombay to take a

B.Sc. degree in chemistry at St Xavier's College.

Subsequently, while employed in Bombay, he studied the Carnatic flute under a now-forgotten teacher and learnt to play the Jaltarangam in the Hindustani manner under Pandit Manohar Barve. He never performed in public. His main aim in learning music was to enjoy himself and gain an understanding of musical theory.

Working as a chemist, Rajagopalan acquired the basic knowledge of pharmaceutical manufacturing. After working in Bombay for four years, he along with his brother L.S. Radhakrishnan started a pharmaceutical manufacturing unit at Trichur. This plant was the source of his livelihood for some forty years, closing down only in the late 1980s after the death of his brother.

At Trichur, Rajagopalan took up studies in Sanskrit and Vedic chanting. Being interested in music, he was trying to understand the musical aspects of Vedic chanting. While looking for various styles of Sāmavedic chanting, he chanced upon the oldest form of the *Kauthuma* branch of Sāmavedic chanting at Puducode village in Palghat district. With very few practitioners, this style had disappeared in other areas. Rajagopalan publicized the existence of this style and was honoured by the Puducode branch of Bharatiya Vidya Bhavan for his effort in 2007.

Rajagopalan's interest in Kūṭiyāṭṭam, Kathakali, Carnatic music and other performing arts of Kerala can be traced back to 1944. He was an active member of the Trichur Kathakali Club and Trichur Sangita Sabha. His friendship with Pandit K.P. Narayana Pisharoti led him to take a deep interest in Kūṭiyāṭṭam. He was later a close friend of masters of Kūṭiyāṭṭam including Mani Madhava Chakyar, Painkulam Rama Chakyar and Ammannur Madhava Chakyar. Foreign scholars would take his help to understand nuances of Kūṭiyāṭṭam. With a fellowship from the A.C. Rangarajan Endowment for Indological Studies administered by the Kuppuswamy Sastri Research Institute, Chennai, Rajagopalan carried out research in Kūṭiyāṭṭam from 1992 to 1994. A monograph on *Women's Role in Kūṭiyāṭṭam*, published by the Institute in 1997, was the fruit of this research. A sequel, *Kūṭiyāṭṭam: Preliminaries and Performance*, was published in 2000. Rajagopalan also contributed the entry on Kūṭiyāṭṭam in the *Oxford Encyclopaedia of Theatre and Performance* edited by Dennis Kennedy (OUP, 2003).

Indigenous musical instruments of Kerala, especially those played in temples, was one of Rajagopalan's strong interests. During the 1960s and 1970s he gave a number of lecture-demonstrations on temple instruments at the annual conferences of the Madras Music Academy. The lectures, published in the *Journal of the Music Academy* ("Thayambaka", 1967; "Thimila", 1971; "Suddha Maddalam", 1972; "Kombu", 1973; "Mizhavu", 1974; "Kurum Kuzhal", 1975; and "Idakka", 1977), have been reproduced in this book. Rajagopalan was at the same time keenly interested in the folk music of Kerala and published several papers on the subject.

With the cooperation of music scholars of Tamil Nadu, Rajagopalan also gave lecture–demonstrations to show how remnants of old Tamil forms still survive in Kerala. Thus he presented the *Kamba-Ramayana* shadow puppetry of Kerala in Madras. Scholars were amazed to see how

Tamil continues to be used in such art forms. Further, Rajagopalan studied Arunachala Kavi's *Rāma Nāṭakam* in Tamil and with the help of M.P. Shankaran Namputhirippad (former Principal of Kerala Kalamandalam), he presented a portion of the *Rāma Nāṭakam* in Kathakali form. He was thus able to demonstrate the close similarity between this work and Kathakali plays. This effort too was well received.

Rajagopalan had worked as a guest lecturer in the Department of Music at Calicut University's Drama Centre in Trichur. He guided many students in writing their dissertations in music at M.A. and Ph.D levels. He also used to evaluate Ph.D theses submitted to the Sankaracharya Sanskrit University, Kalady.

L.S. Rajagopalan was honoured as a guru by the Kerala Sangeetha Nataka Akademi. In 2006, the International Centre for Kudiyattam at Trippunithura presented an award to him for his work in Kūṭiyāṭṭam. In 2007, the Thiruvambady temple of Trichur presented the Maddala Vengichan Gold Medal to him for his work on musical instruments in Kerala's temples. Kerala Kalamandalam bestowed the Kala Ratna award on Rajagopalan in 2006 for research in the performing arts of Kerala.

Rajagopalan had three daughters and one son. His wife Ananthalakshmi passed away in 1999. Up till his death on the 17th of September 2008, Rajagopalan shared his home in Trichur — Lakshmi Niwas, Ganapathy Agraharam — with his son T.R. Subbarayan, his daughter-in-law Lalitha, and his grandson L.S. Rajagopal.

Bibliography

Asan, Ayyippilla, *Rāmakathappāṭṭu* (Malayalam) With an introduction and commentary by P.K. Narayana Pillai, published by author, distributed by National Book Stall, Kottayam, 1970.

Bharatha Iyer, K., *Kathakali: The Sacred Dance-Drama of Malabar*, Luzac, London 1955.

Choondal, Chummar, *Kummāṭṭi* (Malayalam), Published by Kerala Folklore Academy, Trichur, distributed by Kottayam National Book Stall, 1971.

———, *Maṇṇān* (Malayalam), Calicut: Purna Publications, 1979.

———, *Puḷḷuvar̲* (Malayalam), Trivandrum: Charitram Publications, 1981.

———, *Maṇṇān* (Malayalam), Trichur.

———, "Nantuṇi", *Journal of the Music Academy*, Madras, 1975.

———, *Ivar Kaḷi*, Navayugam Weekly, 5 January 1972.

Hariram, Ācharya, *Saṅgīta Damodara* (Śrī Śubhaṅkar viracita), Introduction and tr. into Hindi, Jaipur: Publication Scheme, 1998.

Kothari, K.S., *Indian Folk Musical Instruments*, New Delhi: Sangeet Natak Akademi, 1968.

Krishna Iyer, K. Anantha, *The Tribes and Castes of Cochin*, vol. 1. New Delhi: Cosmo Publications, reprinted 1981.

Krishnaswami, S., *Musical Instruments of India*, Boston: Crescendo Pub. Co., 1971, New Delhi: Publications Division, 1971.

———, *Drums of India*, New Delhi: Publications Division.

———, *Journal of the Music Academy*, vol. xxxviii, pp. 72-82, 1967.

Krishnamurty, S., "Drums of India Through the Ages", *Journal of the Madras Music Academy*, 1987, *Journal of the Madras Music Academy*, 1967.

Kunjunni, Raja, K., *The Contribution of Kerala to Sanskrit Literature*, University of Madras, 1980.

Manmohan, Ghosh, *Nāṭyaśāstra*, tr. and ed. vol. 1, 2nd rev. edn., Calcutta: Manisha Granthalaya, 1967, vol. 2, Asiatic Society 1961.

Menon, C. Achyuta, *Kāḷī-Worship in Kerala*, Madras: University of Madras, 1959.

Rajagopalan, L.S., "Music in Kootiyattam", *Sangeet Natak*, 10, pp. 12-25, 1968.

———, "Musical Instruments of Kerala" (Tamil), 33rd Souvenir, Tamil Isai Sangham, Madras, 1975-76.

———, "Siva Giti", *The Journal of the Madras Music Academy*, vol. xxxvi, pp. 76-87, 1965.

Raghavan, M.D., *Folk Plays and Dances of Kerala*, Published by Rama Varma Archaeological Society, Trichur: The Mangalodayam Press, 1947.

Saṅgīta Ratnākara of Śārṅgadeva, with the *Kalānidhi* of Kallinātha and the *Sudhākara* of Siṁhabhūpāla, ed. S. Subrahmanya Sastri, revised by S. Sarada, Madras: The Adyar Library and Research Centre, 1986.

Sakuntala, K.V., "Martial Musical Instruments of Ancient India", *Sangeet Natak*, 10.

Sambamurthy, P., *South Indian Music*, Books 1-6, 7th edn., Madras: The Indian Music Publishing House, 1968.

———, *Laya Vādyas* (Time-keeping instruments), New Delhi: All India Handicrafts Boards, 1959.

———, *Śruti Vādyas* (Drones), New Delhi: All India Handicrafts Board, 1957.

———, *A Dictionary of South Indian Music and Musicians* (1952), vol. I to VI, Madras: *The Indian Music Publishing House*, rpt. 2001.

Śilappadikāram (Tamil), ed. and published by U.V. Swaminatha Iyer, 1889.

Tantrasamuccaya (Malayalam), Cennās Nārāyaṇan Nampūtirippāt, Commentary by Brahmaśrī Kunnattūr Paṭiññāreṭatt Cerīya Anujan Bhaṭṭatirippāṭ, published by Pañcāṅgam

Pustakaśāla, Kunnamkulam, Kerala, 3rd edn. (ME 1178), 2003.

Venkatrama Iyer, T.L., *Life of Muthuswamy Dikshitar*.

Venkitasubramonia Iyer, S., "Panchavadya", *Journal of the Madras Music Academy*, vol. xxxviii, pp. 136-41, 1967.

———, "Some Rare Tāḷas in Kerala Music," *Sangeet Natak*, 14, 1969.

Index